KEYS TO WORKPLACE SKILLS

How to Get from Your Senior Year to Your First Promotion

KEYS TO WORKPLACE SKILLS

How to Get from Your Senior Year to Your First Promotion

Gary Izumo

Joyce Bishop

Kathleen Cole

Prentice Hall
Upper Saddle River, NJ 07458

Library of Congress Cataloging-in-Publication Data

Izumo, Gary.
    Keys to workplace skills : how to get from your senior year to your first promotion / Gary Isumo, Joyce Bishop, Kathleen Cole.
    p. cm.
  ISBN 0-13-914086-7
    1. Vocational guidance—United States. 2. College graduates—Employment—United States. 3. Job hunting. 4. Career development. I. Bishop, Joyce (Joyce L.), 1950– II. Cole, Kathleen M., 1954– III. Title.
    HF5382.5.U5 I98 1999
    650.14—dc21   98-47210
                                                                                                    CIP
                                                                                                    Rev.

Publisher: *Carol Carter*
Acquisitions Editor: *Sue Bierman*
Managing Editor: *Mary Carnis*
Production: *Holcomb Hathaway, Inc.*
Production Liaison: *Adele Kupchik*
Director of Manufacturing and Production: *Bruce Johnson*
Manufacturing Buyer: *Marc Bove*
Cover Director: *Jane Conte*
Cover Design: *Bruce Kenselaar*
Cover Illustration: *Dana Savoy, SIS, Inc.*
Editorial Assistant: *Michelle M. Williams*
Marketing Manager: *Jeff McIlroy*
Marketing Assistant: *Barbara Rosenberg*

© 1999 by Prentice-Hall, Inc.
A Simon & Schuster Company
Upper Saddle River, New Jersey 07458

All rights reserved. No part of this book may be
reproduced, in any form or by any means,
without permission in writing from the publisher.

Printed in the United States of America

10 9 8 7 6 5 4 3 2 1

ISBN 0-13-914086-7

Prentice-Hall International (UK) Limited, *London*
Prentice-Hall of Australia Pty. Limited, *Sydney*
Prentice-Hall Canada Inc., *Toronto*
Prentice-Hall Hispanoamericana, S.A., *Mexico*
Prentice-Hall of India Private Limited, *New Delhi*
Prentice-Hall of Japan, Inc., *Tokyo*
Simon & Schuster Asia Pte. Ltd., *Singapore*
Editors Prentice-Hall do Brasil, Ltda., *Rio de Janeiro*

Contents

Foreword   xi
Preface   xiii
About the Authors   xv

CHAPTER 1   Taking It to the Next Level:
Understanding Workplace Realities   1

What Can You Expect When You Enter the Working World?   2
  Exciting Changes   2
  Beginnings   3
  Diversity   3
  Responsibilities   3
  Expectations   3

What Basic Skills Can Help You Succeed in Your Career?   4
  Strategic Planning   4
  Time Management   4
  Critical Thinking   5
  Communication   6
  Teamwork   6
  Ethical Development   7

How Can You Make an Effective Transition from College to the Workplace?   7
  Develop Your Skills   7
  Set Deadlines   7
  Be Efficient   8
  Grade Yourself   8
  Continue Your Education   9

IN THE REAL WORLD: Rita Davenport   11
  Develop an Attitude of Achievement   11

Summary   12

Applications & Exercises   13

CHAPTER 2 Bringing Your Dreams to Reality: Goal Setting and Time Management 19

How Do You Set and Achieve Goals? 20
- Personal Goals 20
- Career Goals 21
- Financial Goals 21

How Do You Manage Multiple Goals? 21
- Brainstorm Solutions 22
- Decide Which Solution Is Best 22
- Follow Through with Your Plan 22

How Can You Use a Strategic Plan? 23
- Write a Mission Statement 24
- Put Your Goals in Writing 25
- Analyze Your Strengths and Weaknesses 25
- Analyze the Opportunities and Threats 25
- Reevaluate Your Goals 26
- Develop an Action Plan 26
- Implement Your Plan 27
- Evaluate the Outcome 27

What Tools Can You Use to Accomplish Workplace Objectives? 27
- Goal Setting 27
- Time Management 28
- Strategic Planning 29

IN THE REAL WORLD: Ilene Brody 30

Summary 31

Applications & Exercises 32

CHAPTER 3 Learning Styles: How to Become a Lifelong Learner 39

What Is Your Learning Style? 40
- What Is Your Cognitive Preference? 41

How Can Understanding Your Learning Style Help You Become More Effective and Efficient? 46
- Knowing How You Learn and How You Relate to the World Will Help You Make Smarter Choices 46

IN THE REAL WORLD: Dick Boudreau 47
- You Can Be More Successful on the Job 48
- You Can Become Better at Pinpointing Areas in Which You Need Improvement 48
- You Can Multiple Intelligences to Work 48

Jobs and Learning Styles 49

Summary   51

Applications & Exercises   52

CHAPTER 4 Critical and Creative Thinking:
Expanding Your Mind   57

How Can You Use Critical Thinking Skills to Solve Problems?   58
    Seven Steps for Effective Decision Making   59

How Can You Use Creative Thinking to Make Better Decisions?   63

How Can Creative Thinking Help Solve Problems?   63
    Don't Evaluate or Criticize an Idea Right Away   64
    Focus on Quantity and Worry About Quality Later   64
    Let Yourself Consider Wild and Unorthodox Ideas   64
    Assess Your Creativity   64

What Is Emotional Intelligence and How Can It Help You Become More Effective at Work?   66

IN THE REAL WORLD: John and Carol Newkirk   67
    Empowerment Inventory   68
    Applying the Four Feelings of Empowerment   70
    Self-Mastery   71

Summary   71

Applications & Exercises   73

CHAPTER 5 Expressing Yourself and Understanding Others:
Learning to Communicate Effectively   77

What Are the Basics of Effective Communication?   79
    Think Before You Speak   79
    Be Clear, Precise, and Honest   79
    Communicate within a Reasonable Time Frame   80
    Communicate with Respect   80

How Can You Develop Good Communication Skills?   80
    Develop Listening Skills   80
    Overcome Listening Challenges   81
    Develop Nonverbal Communication Skills   82

IN THE REAL WORLD: Stuart Scott   85

What Are Some of the Barriers to Communication?   85
    Stereotypes   86
    Prejudice   87
    Discrimination   87
    What Can You Do?   87

How Can You Use Good Communication Skills in
   Conflict Resolution?   88
   Dealing With Criticism on the Job   90
Summary   91
Applications & Exercises   92

CHAPTER 6   Effective Workplace Reading:
The Art of Interpreting and Understanding   97

How Can You Improve Your Reading Skills?   99
   Skimming and Scanning   99
   Use the SQ3R Approach   102
How Can You Improve Your Retention of the Material?   105
   Be Aware that Memory Is an Important Part of Your Job   105
   IN THE REAL WORLD: *Merrillyn Shroads*   106
   Use a Mnemonic Device to Boost Your Memory Power   107
   Take Notes as You Read   107
Summary   107
Applications & Exercises   108

CHAPTER 7   Documents:
Communicating Through the Written Word   113

Why Is Good Writing Important to Your Success on the Job?   115
   Words Have Power   116
   Words Trigger Emotions   116
   Words Can Have Different Meanings   117
What Should You Do Before You Begin Writing?   117
   State Your Purpose   117
   Analyze Your Audience   118
   Organize the Content   118
What Are the Elements of the Writing Process?   119
   Develop a Plan   119
   Develop a Draft   120
   Revise   121
   Edit   121
What Documents Are Typically Found in the Workplace?   121
   Business Letters   122
   Memos   123
   E-Mail   123
   Scheduled Reports   124
Summary   125

IN THE REAL WORLD: Robert Pond   126
Applications & Exercises   127

CHAPTER 8 Teamwork and Leadership: Working Effectively with Others   131

Why Are Good Relationships Essential to Your Success?   132

How Can You Participate Effectively as a Member of a Group?   133
- Speak Up When It's Important   134
- Develop Your Creative Thinking Skills   134
- Offer Suggestions, but Try Not to be Invested in Them   134
- Be Discreet   134
- Avoid "Group Think"   135
- Group Conflict   135
- Group Roles   136
- If You Prefer to Lead...   137
- If You Prefer to Participate...   137
- If You Prefer to Negotiate...   137

What Are Leadership Qualities?   138
- Ethics   138

IN THE REAL WORLD: Guy Shafer   139
- Commitment   139
- Creativity   140
- Decisiveness   140
- Initiative   140
- Tenacity   140

Summary   141

Applications & Exercises   142

CHAPTER 9 Taking Care of Personal Business: Managing Your Health and Your Finances   149

How Can You Maintain a Healthy Body?   150
- Think Health   151
- Prioritize   151
- Set Reasonable, Manageable Goals   152

How Can You Nurture a Healthy Mind?   153
- Manage Stress   153
- Manage Your Emotions   155

IN THE REAL WORLD: Paul and Terry Klaassen   156

How Can You Wisely Manage Your Money?   157

    Live Beneath Your Means   *157*
    Pay Yourself   *158*
    Plan Ahead   *158*
  Summary   158

  Applications & Exercises   159

CHAPTER 10   The Road Ahead: Making the Most of Your Career   165

How Do You Achieve Your Lifelong Goals?   167
  Develop a Positive Mind-Set   *167*
  Define Success   *167*
  Have a Plan   *168*
  Think Critically   *168*
  Generate Support   *169*

How Can You Advance Throughout Your Career?   170
  Determine What Your Employer Wants   *170*
  Chronicle Your Successes in Quantifiable Measures   *170*
  Be Realistic   *171*
  Develop Your Skills   *171*
  Ask   *171*

How Can You Manage Failure Effectively?   171

IN THE REAL WORLD: Noel Cunningham   172

Summary   173

Applications & Exercises   174

Closing Thoughts   179

Index   **181**

Foreword

For the past 24 hours, I have been immersed in reading *Keys to Workplace Success*. It was so full of practical, sensible, well-written advice that I wonder why it has taken so long for someone to write a book that provides a virtual step-by-step road map for helping college students prepare for the realities of the world of work. More than ever before, today's college graduates will continue to face new challenges as they enter a workforce that is becoming increasingly more culturally diverse and is changing so rapidly due to technological advancements in telecommunications, computers, and global competition.

Keys to Workplace Success will not only help graduating college students make the transition into the world of work, it also holds very sound advice for those of us who have been in the workforce for some time. I found myself learning a lot while at the same time being engaged by the thought-provoking questions, case studies, and exercises. While reading, I couldn't help but think, "What if there had been a book or a course like this when I graduated from college? How much better prepared would I have been? How many situations at work could I have anticipated? How much trial and error could have been eliminated?"

As you enter the world of work from college, you will also be entering a totally new phase of your life. There's no turning back from here. This is a serious transition and your initial experiences in the workplace and how you handle them will be crucial to giving you the self-confidence you'll need to advance in your chosen career. Although nothing can ever replace actual on-the-job experience, *Keys to Workplace Success* will go a long way in helping you prepare for being successful at work.

This book gives you those strategies necessary to succeed in the workplace and has truly motivated and inspired me, as I'm sure it will you, to succeed in the workplace—and beyond. The strategies are laid out plainly right here for you in black and white. The book covers all of the areas critical to understanding the realities of the workplace. We all owe the authors a great deal of gratitude for taking the time and painstaking research to give us such a well-written book outlining the steps for making this sometimes difficult, but necessary, transition in life much easier to navigate. I hope that your transition into today's workplace is successful and satisfying both personally and professionally as you take your lives to the next level.

Al Wiseman
PRESIDENT, WISEMAN INTERNATIONAL SEMINARS

 **AL WISEMAN,** president and founder of Wiseman International Seminars, is on a mission to help people reach their full potential. As a professional speaker, seminar leader, and sales trainer, he has touched the lives of hundreds of people through his workshops, seminars, and keynote speeches. Born and raised in inner-city Detroit, Al began earning his living in sales as a teenager. He earned his B.S. degree from Wayne State University in business administration, specializing in marketing and sales management. After graduation, he went on to become a top-producing sales and marketing rep for some of America's largest corporations including Unisys and Xerox. A consistently above-quota performer, he was in the top 10% of the sales force and received sales awards and honors at every company he has been affiliated with.

Preface

Every year, thousands of students graduate from college and enter the workforce. Although some students move into their new careers with minimal discomfort, others find themselves in unfamiliar and confusing circumstances. While school is often defined through course syllabi and confined to a campus environment, the world of work can be ambiguous and expansive. Entrants into the workforce may find themselves having to make serious decisions with little or no guidance.

The purpose of this book is to guide you as you make your transition and to help you develop a solid foundation of skills and awareness before you even enter the job market. Each chapter focuses on a different aspect of the world of work. You will learn about:

- workplace realities
- goal setting and time management
- becoming a lifelong learner
- critical and creative thinking
- effective communication, including workplace reading and writing
- teamwork and leadership
- managing your health and personal finances
- making the most of your career

Each chapter contains case studies that encourage problem solving, critical thinking, creative thinking, and brainstorming skills. In addition, there are exercises involving group work, reflective thinking, and personal development. Although these exercises by themselves can be informative, your dedication to applying these skills to your own set of circumstances will be more important than the words you read. You will learn

- how to recognize emotional intelligence in yourself and others
- your dominant learning style and how to apply that to your working style
- how to communicate effectively under any circumstance—even during conflicts
- how to be your own champion by keeping a paper trail of your accomplishments and strengths
- how to meet workplace objectives and still maintain balance in your life
- how to set goals and follow them through to satisfactory completion

Whatever your situation, whether you are just entering the workforce for the first time or entering it as an already seasoned worker, the more you know about today's job market and the expectations of today's employers, the better equipped you will be on your path to success. Use this book and your time within the classroom as an opportunity to increase your career potential. Moreover, use this book as a reference throughout your career whenever you are faced with challenges and transitions or when you need inspiration.

We wish you continued success on your career path!

ACKNOWLEDGMENTS

We would like to thank Lori Martin and Ashleigh Cies for interviewing people for the feature "Real-World Perspectives." Thanks, also, to Stuart Scott, Guy Shafer, Rita Davenport, John Newkirk, Paul and Terry Klaassen, Dick Boudreau, Noel Cunningham, Ilene Brody, Merrillyn Shroads, and Bob Pond for investing their time and effort in contributing the profiles to the book. In addition, we want to thank Kateri Drexler for her outstanding developmental work on the book.

About the Authors

GARY IZUMO is a professor in business at Moorpark College in California and assists large businesses as a management consultant on issues ranging from corporate growth and organizational development, to operational effectiveness. In addition, he writes a monthly business column for the *Los Angeles Times*, Ventura County edition. Gary is an enthusiastic swimmer and reader, but most of all, he enjoys spending time with his family and friends. He believes in contributing to the community and he is an active volunteer to local schools on curriculum and technology matters. Gary is a graduate of Occidental College with a degree in economics and received his MBA from the University of California at Los Angeles.

JOYCE BISHOP holds a Ph.D. in psychology and has taught for more than twenty years, receiving a number of honors, including Teacher of the Year. For the past four years she has been voted "favorite teacher" by the student body and Honor Society at Golden West College in Huntington Beach, California, where she has taught since 1986 and is a tenured professor. She is currently working with a federal grant to establish Learning Communities and  Workplace Learning in her district, and has developed workshops and trained faculty in cooperative learning, active learning, multiple intelligences, workplace relevancy, learning styles, authentic assessment, team building, and the development of learning communities. She also co-authored *Keys to Success*.

KATHLEEN COLE has a strong commitment to helping people realize their unique potential. She has a twenty-five year history as an entertainer, music educator, motivational speaker, and coach. Currently, Kathleen is completing a master's degree in Organizational Leadership and a Master's of Divinity degree. As a trainer and curriculum developer, she has written numerous instructor's manuals and has also worked as a developmental editor on several books. Kathleen currently resides in Lee's Summit, Missouri.

Taking It to the Next Level

Understanding Workplace Realities

KEY CONCEPTS

- What can you expect when you enter the working world?
- What basic skills can help you succeed in your career?
- How can you make an effective transition from college to the workplace?

It is good to have an end to journey toward; but it is the journey that matters, in the end.

Ursula K. Le Guin

Welcome to the beginning of your journey! After studying diligently throughout your education, you are now ready to enter the workplace and actually apply all of those skills you have learned. Or, are you? The working world, as some of you may already know, is quite different in many respects from college life. This book was designed to help you ease into the next phase of your life by developing the skills you will need to create success in whichever field you decide to pursue. You are likely experiencing now what many people in the working world have come to accept as a normal occurrence: *Change*.

Change is inevitable and sometimes can be difficult. With any change comes hesitation (will I fit in?), excitement (I can't wait to meet the people I'm going to be working with), worry (what if I can't do the job?), or any combination of emotions. No matter what you're feeling about the changes in your life at this time, by taking an active part now in deciding your future, you will build a base that will help you manage change throughout your life. This is the beginning of a wonderful adventure—one in which you have the starring role. By carefully planning how you will approach the change, you can make the transition pleasant and rewarding.

The foundation of workplace success is found in the strategy that you set for your life. Every person has different interests, abilities, and motivations. Finding what drives and inspires you will make the difference in your overall life success. Chapter 2 presents guidelines that help set strategies and goals. This will be the basis for all of the skill development found throughout this book.

In this chapter the ways in which the workplace is different from school are explored. We will also discuss skills that will likely be important as you go through your career, and we will look at how to make an effective transition into the workplace. Getting the job is the easy part, but having a job takes a lot of work!

WHAT CAN YOU EXPECT WHEN YOU ENTER THE WORKING WORLD?

Many things will be different in this next phase of your life. Some of the differences you may expect, but other differences may surprise you. Understanding as much as possible about what you will encounter can help you thrive in your new environment.

Exciting Changes

The Chinese symbol for change actually has two meanings. One is *chaos* and the other is *opportunity*. The character communicates that every challenging, demanding, and chaotic situation in life also presents a wonderful opportunity. By meeting the challenge in a positive manner, you can discover the good that this change holds for you.

Change can be exciting! You will meet new people, learn a great deal, and accomplish much. We are seeing enormous and far-reaching changes in our world today. With so much information available and so many advances being made, we need always to be prepared for changes and the anxiety that goes along with them. In many industries companies are streamlining their business—they do not have as many employees as they once did. Current employees are thus having to do more with less, and they are having to use their creativity to deal with these challenges.

Beginnings

For some of you, this may be the first time in your life that an end is not in sight! There are no graduations ahead. Certainly, you will have promotions and job changes, but there is no final goal unless you, yourself, set one. There is not a syllabus to follow. You will be the only person responsible for your future. This can be tremendously empowering, or a little intimidating, but throughout the book we will show you how to manage this responsibility. Remember: *In order to be successful, you must take responsibility for your life.*

Diversity

We have seen organizations become much more diverse in recent years—in culture, education, age, and gender. Women represented 40 percent of the workforce in 1976, but that number is estimated to grow to 47 percent by the year 2000. In addition, there are increasing opportunities for women. The percentage of women in managerial positions in the U.S. increased from 15 percent in 1990 to 40 percent in 1996. Minorities are expected to account for over 30 percent of the new entrants in the U.S. workforce by 2000. The average employee is also getting older. In the United States, the median age was 27 in 1970, but is projected to reach 39 by the year 2000.

The working world will expose you to all kinds of human differences in ethnicity, culture, religion, ability, and more. This diversity presents many opportunities for learning about and understanding people, but it also presents many challenges. Communication and team-building skills are becoming increasingly important, and leadership skills now involve managing a diverse workforce. Understanding that people are different, and motivated by different factors, is critical to success in the workplace today.

Responsibilities

One of the biggest surprises to new entrants in the workforce is that they are not given much responsibility at first. This can be disheartening, especially if you believe the organization can run more smoothly if your changes are implemented. Use this time, when you have fewer responsibilities, to learn as much as possible. Ask a lot of questions, meet a lot of people, and give yourself some time before making suggestions. If you are in a field that you like, concentrate on doing the best job possible in the short term—no matter what your duties. Your responsibilities will quickly increase.

Expectations

You might encounter a higher performing group of people on the job, overall, than you found in school. Many people have been working for some time and have gained knowledge specific to the field. Because of this, you will likely find that greater expectations are put on you. Even if you don't have decision-making authority, you will probably still be expected to provide high-quality work.

WHAT BASIC SKILLS CAN HELP YOU SUCCEED IN YOUR CAREER?

As you embark on your new career, you will probably already have solid skills in some areas that will help you succeed in the workplace. Other skills may need a lot of refinement, but skill development is a continuing process. Some of the important skills you will use throughout your career include strategic planning, time management, critical thinking, communication, teamwork, and ethical development. Different positions will emphasize different skills, so it is important to understand the different careers and their requirements.

Strategic Planning

Successful people don't just let life just happen to them. They spend time shaping and molding the dreams that matter. Creating a vision for yourself, spending time defining goals that will culminate in that vision, planning ways to accomplish those goals, and taking action are the building blocks of success.

The ability to set priorities will be very important in determining goals for your career. Likewise, these will be important for prioritizing your short-term goals. Your personal strategic plan will ultimately be the guideline for how you prioritize your duties on a daily basis. Chapter 2 will help you set your strategy, goals, and plan of action.

Time Management

Your time is about to become a more valuable resource. Because it is limited, make the most of it on a daily, monthly, yearly, and lifetime basis. Setting priorities in advance will help manage your time, but, like many skills, this ability can always be refined and improved.

Some people entering the workforce have trouble adjusting to the work schedule. In college if you're late for class, or even miss a class altogether, the consequences are relatively light. The professor may ask you to submit an extra assignment, or you may have to call another student to get the day's notes. All in all, it's not too harmful if you miss a class or two. If you miss work, however, you let down the other employees who are counting on you to do your part. You also let down your employer. If you're working on a big project, your tardiness or absence may cost the company large sums of money. Be sure and show up regularly and on time. The cost of covering for you may not be worth it to your manager and peers, and you could lose your job. Make timeliness a priority.

There are some actions that you can take that may help you get adjusted to working full-time. These include the following:

Plan ahead. Decide what you're going to wear to work the night before. Fill the gas tank the day before when you have time—waiting until the morning may delay you unnecessarily. If you take the bus or another form of transit, make sure you have a pass or the correct change. You don't want to be scrambling for a cash machine early in the morning.

Change your habits. If you like to stay up late and watch old movies, now is a great time to start taping the shows and watching them on the weekend while you have the time. If you like to get together with friends during the week, make sure you're giving yourself enough time for sleep. If you're burning the candle at both ends, you might end up making mistakes at work that could cost you a promotion, or even your job.

Develop new routines. If you're used to exercising in the evening, why not try it early in the morning? You may like the extra energy it gives you as you begin your day. Maybe you could get up an hour earlier and head off to the local coffee house for a latté and a look at the *New York Times*. Or you could even arrive at work an hour earlier than you're scheduled in order to write your daily "To Do" list or catch up on trade magazines. Whatever you decide you would like to do, now is an optimum time to establish new and effective routines for yourself.

Use a calendar or a daytimer. Many successful business people use a daytimer to help organize their commitments and activities. Use it to keep track of appointments, phone calls you have to make, projects you have to finish, promises you've made to others, and anything else that you want to remember.

Critical Thinking

With all of the information available today, it is very important to be able to quickly go though it and determine its value. In college you've taken multiple choice and true/false exams. You learned that there were right and wrong answers. You learned which chemicals make certain products, how to use computer programs, which historical events shape our lives, and how to write an effective essay. Even though you probably have been asked to analyze topics from differing perspectives, much of undergraduate work has definite answers and objectives. It can seem like there are black and white responses to every situation.

This is not so, though, in the working world. There are so many shades of gray that at times it can be difficult to decide which path is the best one to take. You'll need to learn to think critically about the tasks and decisions you make on the job. Later on in this book, you'll have the chance to take an in-depth look at effective reasoning skills. For now, here are a few general tips for effective reasoning:

Brainstorm solutions. When you need to make a decision, whether it be which person to assign to a task, how to motivate an employee, or what steps to take toward accomplishing monthly targets, brainstorm a list of possible solutions. For every idea look at the pros and cons. Then decide which solution looks best.

Think outside the box. Use your creative thinking skills to find solutions to everyday workplace situations and demands. Take a look at the big picture—what your department is focused on accomplishing and how it applies to the company as a whole. Imagine what the company would be like if you had unlimited resources to help it achieve its goals. What would you do? Would you purchase new equipment? Hire another professional? Get training? Just by letting your thoughts roam, you can often come up with practical, effective ideas that will benefit the company.

Explore different perspectives. In the working world, you are going to meet people who have thoughts, behaviors, and beliefs that are different from your own. An important part of work is learning to get along with others. Learn to see things from another's perspective. Try and understand what makes them tick—or gets them ticked off! Then learn to work with their particular personality.

Communication

Successful communication in a diverse workplace requires skills in several areas. Listening, reading, writing, and verbal and nonverbal skills are critical to achieving workplace success.

Conflict resolution is also a skill you will frequently use throughout your career. Along with the communication basics that are discussed in the text, techniques for resolving different types of conflict are examined.

In a study involving several companies conducted in the early 1990s, it was found that people who spent a larger percentage of their time networking were more likely to get promoted. The concept is simple enough—as you meet more people, who also know more people, you expand your list of contacts. It is important, as you continue through your career, to keep an organized list of the people you meet and to try to expand this base. There are several ways you can accomplish this:

- Join professional associations.
- Volunteer in the community.
- Participate in community events.
- Join team sports.
- Explore other interests.

Teamwork

Group work is becoming more and more important in today's workplace. As businesses continue to change and develop, this trend will continue. Teamwork will become much more of a critical element to workplace success. However, it is still an underdeveloped skill in most individuals within American society.

Most groups go through several stages. After a group is formed, members of the group will jockey for position—for instance, some members may want to be leaders while others may want to avoid having more demands placed on them. Only after the group members settle into their roles will the group actually perform. The trick is to minimize the time spent struggling so the group can quickly move on to being productive.

Ethical Development

Throughout your career, you will be faced with daily decisions and choices. Through these choices, your ethical framework will be molded. In today's world, a clear delineation between right and wrong, or good and bad, does not always exist so it becomes important to have guidelines to follow. For instance, if you were in charge of marketing research for your company, would it be proper to hire a spy to infiltrate your competitor? What if somebody came to you and offered to sell you information? What if you met one of your competitors at a social event who did not know you were in marketing research? Would it be ethical to keep that information to yourself while speaking with him or her about business issues?

We often have ethical dilemmas because we are concentrating on short-term gains. By stepping back and looking at the larger picture, sometimes we are able to set and keep higher standards for ourselves. If you did identify yourself at the social event, for example, you will always be trusted by your competitor, which may come in handy some day if, as they frequently do, your two companies merge! If you live by the highest standards possible, the long-term gains will outstrip the sum of the short-term gains.

HOW CAN YOU MAKE AN EFFECTIVE TRANSITION FROM COLLEGE TO THE WORKPLACE?

Develop Your Skills

As you go through this book and the course, identify areas in which you would like to see improvement. Develop a plan for improving these skills and set the plan into action. The following chapters will provide guidelines and suggestions, but the work belongs to you. Changing habits usually takes twenty-one days, so be patient! Develop your plan, break it down into manageable pieces, and keep moving in the direction of your goal.

Set Deadlines

Most jobs demand that the employee take responsibility for their own behavior. Unless your supervisor believes in micromanagement, by which every detail of your job is closely monitored, you will be expected to set daily and monthly goals for yourself and have the ability to regularly meet those goals. Although your duties will more than likely be defined by a job description, the projects that are yours to complete will depend on your creating and sticking to deadlines.

Be Efficient

By being efficient with all of your resources, you will be able to accomplish more and stay on task. Suggestions for ways in which to do this follow.

Organize. The more organized you can make your work area, the better. Clutter can slow you down. Many hours are lost just looking through piles of paper for the one that's needed. If you can't easily locate the figures, dimensions, budget, or contacts requested by your boss, you're not going to be very efficient. Spend time each morning organizing your work area and your day. Spend a few minutes before you go home organizing your desk and filing papers.

Keep a to-do list. Begin your day with a list of the tasks you want to or need to accomplish. Highlight the items that absolutely must be done.

Use a desk calendar. It's helpful to be able to look at your month all at once. After you've established your monthly goals, advise your supervisor what you have planned for the month. They'll appreciate the initiative.

Use time efficiently. Developing healthy workplace relationships is an important part of everyone's job. Make sure, though, that the relationships are not more important than getting the work done. If you find yourself chatting when you should be working, excuse yourself and get back on the job. If others keep popping by your desk to chat, make arrangements to continue the conversation over lunch or after work.

Grade Yourself

Taking responsibility for your life and success will mean consistently analyzing, or grading, yourself. For those of you who have already held a job, or have begun the interviewing process, you have probably spent some time considering your strengths and weaknesses. Self-evaluation, however, is not just about getting hired; it is tied to all aspects of your career.

Throughout your employment, whether formally or informally, you will always be evaluated. Although formal performance appraisals may be uncomfortable, understanding what to expect beforehand and knowing your own strengths and weaknesses, will put you in an advantageous position. Remember, though, you're your own scorekeeper. Don't expect your employer to do this for you. Take charge and regularly evaluate yourself against your own expectations. It is very important to keep a paper trail of your accomplishments. Among other attributes and achievements, you may want to evaluate the following:

Ability to manage objectives. Objectives are set in a variety of ways, depending on the philosophy of the company. Sometimes they are set in the traditional top-down way, with companywide goals and objectives coming from top management. These are then broken down into department and individual objectives through middle and line managers. Other companies may use an MBO (Management by Objectives) approach, whereby the employees and their managers jointly set the objectives.

Your employers will be primarily interested in knowing whether or not you are able to accomplish your objectives. They will place a lot of importance on your end results. For instance, if your job demands that you produce 500 widgets an hour with a 1 percent margin of error and you produce 550 widgets an hour with only a half-percent error, your rating will be above average. On the other hand, if you're expected to land three new advertising accounts a month and you land only one, your performance rating will be below average.

You may find that you have conflicting objectives—your manager may want you to accomplish two tasks, but only allow you time to finish one. Or you might have assignments from two different managers that conflict with each other. If this happens, you will have to ask your immediate supervisor to prioritize the projects or assignments.

Ability to respond to customer's needs. Do you understand the needs of your clients? Are you attending to customer priorities while at the same time providing solutions when delays or problems arise?

Ability to work with others. Look at the way that you interact with others when you need to work in groups. Is this an area in which you need improvement? What can you do to improve your teamwork skills?

Ability to effectively communicate. How well do you convey yourself. Do you write and speak clearly? Do you mean what you say? Are you able to influence, inspire, or critique others?

Ability to self-manage. Are you able to work alone and complete projects with little guidance? Can you set goals for yourself and meet them? Do you anticipate problems and work out possible solutions ahead of time?

Ability to handle the technical aspects of the job. Are you able to handle the technical aspects of your job? Do you stay informed about innovations in your field? Are you competent, skilled, informed, and able to deliver?

Continue Your Education

Never before have the advances of the world exploded at such a rapid-fire pace. Technologies of today will more than likely be obsolete in a few years. Global communication, once thought to be impossible, is the norm. Cultures that were once isolated are now integrating into the business and world communities. The more you can stay informed about the changes, the better chance you have of not only adapting to the change but guiding others to do the same.

Besides keeping you up to date with the changes and improving your quality of life, continued education can greatly increase your income. The U. S. Department of Commerce Census Report shows that people who receive an education beyond high school can add approximately ten thousand dollars to their salary for every two additional years of education. For example, if the average high school graduate earned $10,000 a year; a person with their associate's degree would likely earn $20,000 a year; a bachelor's degree could earn, on average, $40,000 a year, and so forth.

In addition to the financial benefits, lifelong learning does the following:

Expands your self-confidence. As you rise to the challenge of learning new things, you will discover that your capacity for knowledge and personal growth is greater than you imagined.

Increases your possibilities. More opportunities, on and off the job, open for you when you build your skill levels.

Improves your personal health. The smarter you become about the choices you make, the better chance you will have at living a healthy life. People who learn about the danger of certain choices are more likely to avoid them.

Improves your community and world. Informed people recognize their role in the larger picture and usually can't help but get involved.

You can continue learning throughout your life by using some of these suggestions:

Read, read, read. People who stay informed on current events, new technologies, and trends have a better chance of adapting to the changes when they arrive. And you can be a reference for helping others adapt—something employers will really appreciate.

Attend seminars and in-house training sessions and take courses. The more you know about effective communication, techniques in problem solving, managing conflict and change, and motivation theories, the more effective you will be on the job. Find ways to regularly hone your interpersonal skills.

Study different cultures. Keep your eyes open for workshops, seminars, and information about other cultures. The more you know about customs, communication styles, and cultural issues, the better able you will be to work with employees from different cultures and the more knowledgeable you will be about countries with which your company interacts.

Access on-line information. Increasingly, people who wish to access pertinent information are using the Internet and its resources. Get your home computer on-line and use it to browse the services of your competition or to learn more about the global market.

IN THE REAL WORLD: RITA DAVENPORT

Rita Davenport has been the CEO of Arbonne, a company that markets nutrition and personal care products, for the past three years. And she's done it from home.

It seems too good to be true, but Rita has brought corporate headquarters to her front door. Arbonne sales now reach approximately $35 million, and are only expected to increase. So who is this woman? Where did she come from? And how did she manage to secure the type of job most people only dream about?

Rita Davenport grew up in Phoenix, Arizona. From the low-income side of town, she managed to work her way into the media as a local television celebrity. Along the way she began to distribute Arbonne's products, and before she realized it, she was one of Arbonne's top distributors. "After speaking at one of the company's events, I decided to sign up myself in 1989. I paid $50 dollars for my starter kit and have done pretty well," she says.

Just two years later, Arbonne took Rita Davenport to the top, offering her the chance to test her sales ability in a multimillion dollar corporation, as president of the company. After evaluating the job, Davenport determined that her success was partially due to the freedom she had working at home. She worked for Arbonne because it allowed her flexibility. All that would change if she worked in an office. She argued that she could excel at the position from her house in Phoenix, where she was happy. Eventually, Arbonne saw it Rita's way.

> I love the way Arbonne's network marketing motivates people. Imagine, in a corporation, if you were told that you would get a raise when everyone working for you gets a raise. Imagine how helpful, understanding, and tolerant you would be. Imagine how supportive and dedicated your employees would be—because your success depends on their success. That's what is unique about our business. It's not "dog-eat-dog." That's what I love about the business.

Rita Davenport has definitely proven that almost anyone can change careers, make more money, face adversity, and come out on top. Sometimes you don't find a niche, a niche finds you!

Learning is more than the process of going to school and earning a degree or certificate. It is a choice to improve your mind and your skills. If you make the most of your mind, your time, and your educational opportunities, you will realize your potential. *Keep an open mind!*

Develop an Attitude of Achievement

Probably one of the qualities an employer will find the most appealing is an attitude of achievement. This attitude affects everything you do: how you dress, how you respond to change, how you accept constructive criticism, and how well you complete your objectives. If you have an attitude that is agreeable and cooperative, people will want you on their team.

SUMMARY

*The credit belongs to the one who strives valiantly;
who comes up short again and again;
who knows great enthusiasm and great devotion;
who spends himself in a worthy cause;
and who, at the best, knows in the end the triumph of high achievement;
and who, at worst, if he fails, at least fails while daring greatly,
so that his place shall never be with those timid souls
who know neither victory nor defeat.*

Theodore Roosevelt

Though no one book, person, or class can turn everything around and make it happen for you, this book, and the other resources your school offers, can provide suggestions and support. When making decisions about your future, make choices that make sense for your unique and individual needs.

The world is changing, as is the workplace. This change should continue to occur at a rapid pace, and being successful in the working world will require adjustment to this continual change. You will be the only person responsible for your future success, and you won't have guidelines to follow unless you set them for yourself. The working world will be more diverse, in terms of race, ethnicity, age, religion, and abilities, which will present opportunities as well as challenges. Although you will probably not be given a lot of responsibility or decision-making authority at the beginning of your career, there will be greater expectations placed on you because you'll be among an overall higher performing group of people.

Strategic planning, time management, critical thinking, communication, teamwork, and ethical development are skills that will help in your career success. Different jobs will require different skills, and skill development is a life-long pursuit.

Building a professional life takes continual learning. The more you engage in the learning process—by staying aware, flexible, and open—the better chance you have of achieving your lifelong goals. Continue learning throughout your career and promote an attitude of achievement in all that you do.

Applications & Exercises

1.1 Self-Evaluation

In the following exercise you will have the opportunity to evaluate your performance at school. Begin by thinking about your general grade point average. Then reflect on your quality of work during the course of your education. Did it leave something to be desired? Did you give it your best? Did you seek out help when you needed it?

Read each item below and then circle the number that best describes your performance.

1. **Knowledge:** What degree of knowledge have you gained in your different subjects? Would you consider yourself an expert? Do you show interest in learning more?

    Below Average   *Average*   *Above Average*
    1   2   3   4   5   6   7   8   9

2. **Quality of Work:** What attention do you give to your work? Do you check spelling? Have others proofread for you? Turn papers in when they're due? Rework them if they're below par?

    Below Average   *Average*   *Above Average*
    1   2   3   4   5   6   7   8   9

3. **Quantity of Work:** Do you give more than is expected? Are you able to help others with their commitments? Do you help out in the classroom? Volunteer regularly?

    Below Average   *Average*   *Above Average*
    1   2   3   4   5   6   7   8   9

4. **Attendance and Punctuality:** Do you arrive on time and are you well prepared? If absent, do you inform those who need to know and ask for help making up the time?

    Below Average   *Average*   *Above Average*
    1   2   3   4   5   6   7   8   9

5. **Flexibility:** Do you like working as a member of a team? Do you find it easy to change when the situation calls for it. Do you respect other's opinions? Do you stand up for your own opinion when it matters?

    Below Average   *Average*   *Above Average*
    1   2   3   4   5   6   7   8   9

6. **Initiative:** Do you use your imagination? Are you comfortable making decisions? Can you originate and develop new ideas?

    Below Average   *Average*   *Above Average*
    1   2   3   4   5   6   7   8   9

7. **Planning and Organizing:** Here you show whether you are able to define objectives and set steps to meeting them. How well do you organize your papers? Are you able to stick to your plans? Do you use different resources to accomplish your goals?

   Below Average　　　　　　　*Average*　　　　　　　*Above Average*
   　1　　2　　3　　4　　5　　6　　7　　8　　9

8. **Ethics:** Do you reference other people's work? Do you use your own material? Do you write fresh material or do you draw on papers you've already written? Do you tell the truth about why your paper's late or why you weren't able to finish your part on a group project? How honest are you?

   Below Average　　　　　　　*Average*　　　　　　　*Above Average*
   　1　　2　　3　　4　　5　　6　　7　　8　　9

PERSONAL ASSETS

Employee Expectations

Besides knowing what the employer expects from you on the job, it's important to understand your own expectations. Think about what you want from your employer. You might feel that time off for the care of sick children is important. You may feel that the ability to advance is crucial to your goals. You may feel a support system that can train you during the beginning months of your job is essential. Perhaps you want to work in an informal environment. Whatever is important to you on the job, take the time to identify it and find methods for achieving your desires. If you find that your expectations cannot be met, decide if you should live with things the way they are, wait patiently in the hope that things will change, or take steps to look for better circumstances.

Describe the perfect job. What makes it perfect? Think about the aspects of that job as you determine what it is that you need from your employer.

1. It is important to me that my employer provide

   _____

   I might ensure this by

   _____
   _____
   _____

   If the expectation cannot be met, I would

   _____
   _____
   _____

2. I would also like
   _____
   _____

   I might meet this expectation by
   _____
   _____
   _____

   If the expectation cannot be met, I would
   _____
   _____
   _____

3. I expect to work in an environment that is
   _____
   _____

   I might meet this expectation by
   _____
   _____
   _____

   If the expectation cannot be met, I would
   _____
   _____
   _____

4. I expect
   _____
   _____

   I might meet this expectation by
   _____
   _____
   _____

   If the expectation cannot be met, I would
   _____
   _____
   _____

WORKING TOGETHER

Learning from Others

Much of your work in the business field will involve other people. Your ability to work well with others affects promotions and job performance. Use these group exercises as an opportunity to hone your group skills. Make sure you're actively participating in the projects, listening and respecting each other's opinions, contributing your own ideas, and doing your share of the work.

In the following exercise, you will need to break into groups of three to five people, and identify business leaders or managers whom your group can interview (each person should interview one manager). Your group's assignment is to discover what today's managers are saying about success. You might ask the managers "What qualities do you consider important for success?" "Why are these qualities so important?" "What is the single-most important attribute you look for in a job candidate?"

Once your group has decided who will be interviewed and what questions will be asked, gather the information and report back to the class.

CASE STUDIES

What Would You Do?

One

Tom had only been on the job for two months when he discovered that his coworker, Mandy, was stealing from the company. At first, he wasn't too concerned because it was just little items like a ream of paper or a box of pencils. After a while, though, he became more and more frustrated with the situation. He realized she was using the copy machine for personal copies and company time to make personal phone calls.

Tom really didn't feel he'd been working there long enough to get involved, yet her stealing went against his moral fiber. What can he do? On a separate piece of paper, use brainstorming techniques to develop a list of possible solutions and the possible consequences of choosing each solution. When you are finished, discuss the options with the rest of the class.

Two

Imagine that you have just turned in a month-end report and it came back to your desk covered in red marks. You're very upset because you worked hours on it and felt it was perfect. How are you going to deal with it? How will you deal with your disappointment? Brainstorm a list of ways you can handle the situation. Discuss your ideas with the rest of the class.

Three

Sarah always seemed to run a few minutes behind for everything. In school it really didn't matter because most of her classes allowed a few minutes for people to settle in before the lecture or discussion began. Sarah's friends knew she was reliable and would eventually show up to their functions. They didn't mind her being late. At least she didn't think so. It wasn't until she started her job that her habit became a real problem. At first, she arrived right at 8:00 A.M. Then as she became more relaxed about her job, she began to get careless about arriving on time. Soon, she was arriving at five minutes after the hour, then ten minutes, and sometimes even fifteen minutes later than her scheduled time. Usually she rushed in with an excuse about traffic, threw her coat over her chair, and began working. Sometimes she would tell her boss that she would deduct the time from her first break or her lunch hour.

After Sarah had been at her job for two months she was fired. The supervisor explained that she didn't have an appropriate commitment to her job. Sarah felt that they should have given her a warning so she could have the chance to mend her ways. What do you think?

1. Should the manager have given Sarah the chance to change her habits? Why or why not?

2. Does the manager "owe" Sarah the chance to prove herself on the job? Why or why not?

3. What steps would you recommend Sarah take to help her succeed on her next job?

Bringing Your Dreams to Reality

Goal Setting and Time Management

KEY CONCEPTS

- How do you set and achieve goals?
- How do you manage multiple goals?
- How can you use a strategic plan?
- What tools can you use to accomplish workplace objectives?

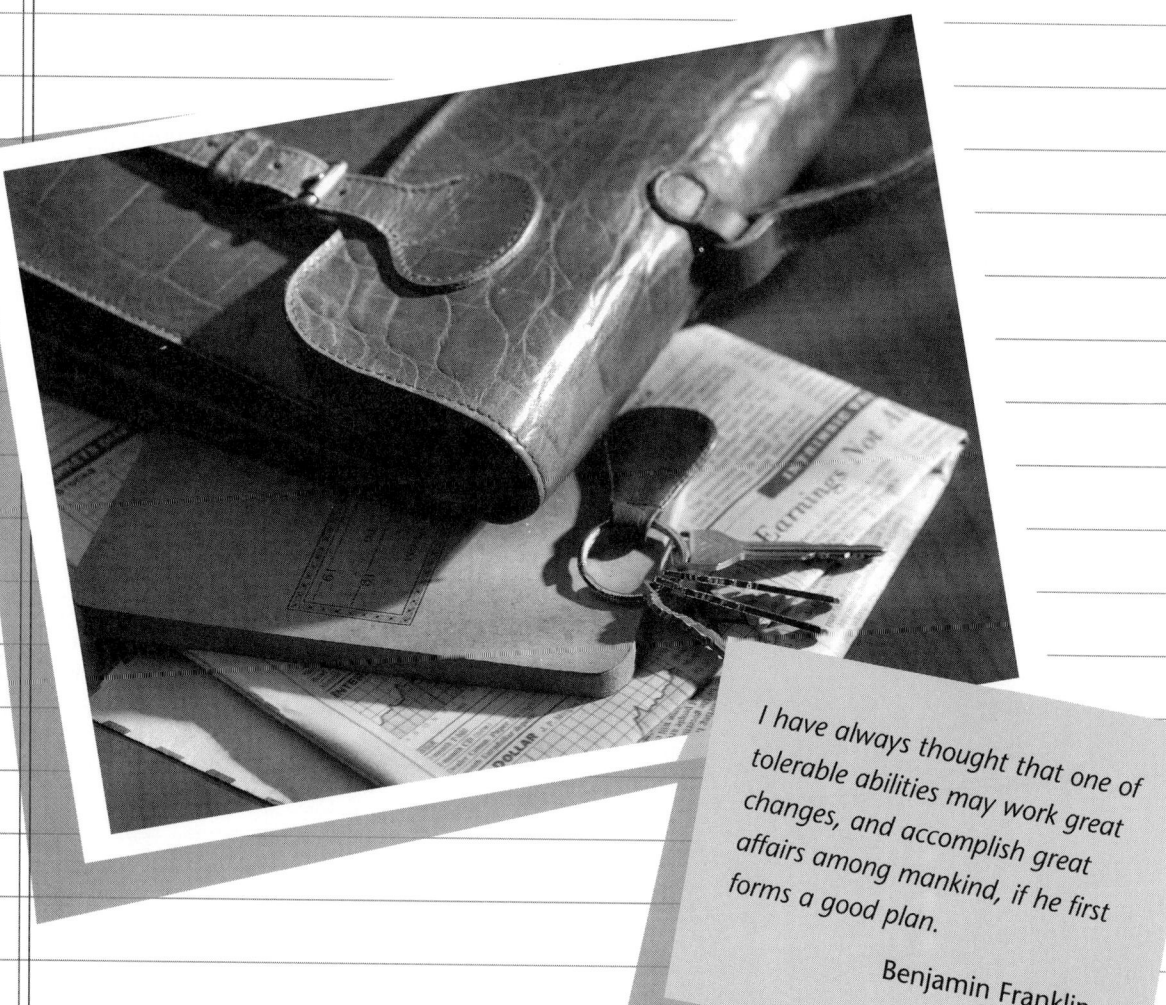

I have always thought that one of tolerable abilities may work great changes, and accomplish great affairs among mankind, if he first forms a good plan.

Benjamin Franklin

There are, literally, thousands of career paths available to take, and you could choose from any of these or even make your own path. Though picking a career from the many choices may seem like a daunting task, it doesn't have to be. If you first determine what you want out of your life, your career decisions become much easier to make. Knowing how to set goals and meet them is an important skill to have for career and life success. Just as every skill requires some degree of practice, you'll also need to practice setting goals to make the most of your time and energy.

Determining what your goals are, and developing a strategic plan for your life, takes some work, but it's well worth the effort. Besides helping to prioritize aspects of your life, your plan will show your employers that you are a person who can prioritize objectives. This skill is critical in today's changing workplace where time is a very important commodity, and spending it doing the most important tasks is crucial.

HOW DO YOU SET AND ACHIEVE GOALS?

What are goals? How do they differ from dreams? Generally speaking, both goals and dreams are ideas for our lives that we would like to fulfill. The main difference between goals and dreams is that goals have a definite time frame. A goal can be something as concrete as getting promoted or as abstract as working to control your temper. When you set goals and work to achieve them, you engage your intelligence, abilities, time, and energy to get ahead. Most of us have already set goals and are working toward their completion. Sometimes there may be several ways of accomplishing the same goal and you'll have to choose among alternatives. Goal setting can become difficult when there are several conflicting objectives.

Goals can be addressed from several different perspectives. You can set goals according to time (long-term and short-term goals), according to life areas (i.e., personal, career, financial), and according to importance. No matter how you define and order your goals, the most important piece of the equation is to make sure your goals reflect your values.

Personal Goals

In this section, reflect on what you want in your personal life. Think about how you want to develop as a person. What goals do you have for yourself? Do you want to live in the city? Do you want to travel or stay close to home? Do you want to be married or stay single? Do you want children? Do you want to live close to relatives? Use the following section as an opportunity to identify your personal goals.

In addition to the above, ask yourself:

- Do you want to gain knowledge?
- Do you want more confidence?
- Do you want to be physically fit?
- Do you want to be a better time manager?

- What do you want to do in your leisure time?
- How will you give back to your community?

Career Goals

Consider the job requirements, job duties, hours, co-workers, salary, transportation to and from the office, amount of travel, and company size and style that might be associated with your ideal job. Start thinking also about what it will take to have the kind of job you want and what steps you'll need to take to get there. Furthermore, think about how you want to advance along your career path. Will you need more training or certification to advance? Where would you like to be in your job one year from now? Five years? Ten years?

In addition, ask yourself:

- What skills do I want to use on a daily basis?
- How much responsibility do I want?
- What kinds of benefits are important to me?
- How will I be a lifelong learner?

Your career goals will impact the choices you make in your personal life and vice versa. For instance, you may want a job that initially requires a great deal of travel. At the same time, your spouse may have just started a new job that demands a great deal of overtime work. Both of you will need to decide if your relationship or the welfare of the children can withstand your schedules.

Financial Goals

Financial goals affect the career you choose, the type of education you desire, and the development of a family. Compare your current financial picture and set goals that will help you bridge the gap between where you are now and where you want to be in the future.

Ask yourself:

- How much money do I need to cover living expenses?
- What kind of money will it take for the type of lifestyle I'm seeking?
- How much money do I want to have in savings?
- Will I need to borrow money for a home? A car?
- How much is my education going to cost me?

HOW DO YOU MANAGE MULTIPLE GOALS?

One of the most difficult challenges we face when trying to meet goals is deciding how to keep the different parts of our lives balanced and integrated. Learning how to fit goals together takes skill. On any given day, the demands of your job may interfere with the demands of your personal life. For instance, you may need to pick up your son or daughter from the childcare center no later than six o'clock, but your boss wants you to stay late and finish the report that's needed for tomorrow morning's presentation.

You have to weigh the priorities, brainstorm solutions, decide which solution is best, and follow through with your plan. But what if both goals are equally important? In this case, you could arrange for a friend or family member to pick up your child and watch him or her until you are finished with your report. Or you could take the report home with you and finish it in the evening. You could also pick up your child on time, take him to a sitter, and come back to the office to finish your work. Use the following tips for managing conflicting goals.

Brainstorm Solutions

When faced with conflicting goals, take out a pad of paper and write down as many options for resolving the problem as you can. Let your brain find solutions no matter how ridiculous they may sound at the moment. Don't evaluate them yet. Just let the ideas flow. You'll be surprised at how many options you really have.

Suppose you have met someone in your department that you want to start dating. The feeling is mutual but you are both very aware of the no dating policy of your company. You both brainstorm possible solutions . . .

> You could quit your job.
> The other person could quit or move to a different division.
> You could decide not to pursue the relationship.
> You could stay friends for now and make a decision at a later time.
> You could discuss the situation with your boss.
> You could try to keep the relationship secret.

Decide Which Solution Is Best

Now you can evaluate which decision is best by weighing the consequences of each idea. For instance, say you decide to keep the relationship secret. What will you do if you're discovered dining out together or having an affectionate moment outside the office? If you quit your job, how will you provide for yourself? How easy or difficult will it be to find other work in your field? How will it look on your resume? Weigh the consequences and then decide your course of action.

Follow Through with Your Plan

In the preceding situation, the two employees may have decided to wait a few months and see if their feelings were legitimate before making any career moves. They may agree to reopen the discussion at a later date. Stephen Covey, author of the best selling books *The Seven Habits of Highly Effective People* and *First Things First*, writes:

Putting first things first is an issue at the very heart of life. Almost all of us feel torn by the things we want to do, by the demands placed on us, by the many responsibilities we have. We all feel challenged by the day to day and moment-by-moment decisions we must make regarding the best use of our time. Decisions are easier when it's a question of "good" or "bad." We can easily see how some ways we could spend our time are wasteful, mind-numbing, even destructive. But for most of us, the issue is not between good and bad, but between good and "best." So often, the enemy of the best is the good.

Learning how to balance all the activities of your day can be a demanding task. One effective way is to list your daily activities according to importance. Look at the following chart of priorities. One is a list from a returning adult student. As you can see, she has different obligations than the traditional student.

Figure 2.1 *Two students compare priorities.*

RETURNING ADULT STUDENT	PRIORITIES	TRADITIONAL AGE STUDENT	PRIORITIES
Caring for my daughter	(1) Family	Classes and studying	(1) Education
Working at my job	(2) Work	Friends	(2) Relationships
Studying, classes	(3) Education	Working out	(3) Health
Relationships	(4) Relationships	Part-time job	(4) Work
Household tasks	(5) Household	Volleyball team	(5) Sports
Personal time and wellness	(6) Renewal	Movies	(6) Entertainment
Church and meditation	(7) Spiritual life	Chores, errands	(7) Household

Another important part of goal clarification is to determine how your goals connect to one another. If your long-term goal is to become a manager, your immediate goal may be to find out what the job entails. Once you have that information, you might want to declare your intention to your supervisor and ask for help in accomplishing your goal. Next, you might want to meet with your mentor, or someone whose opinion you respect, to examine your strengths and weaknesses for the potential position. Breaking large goals into minor goals, or objectives, is a very important part of goal setting. A personal strategic plan can help immensely.

HOW CAN YOU USE A STRATEGIC PLAN?

If you've ever played a game of chess or checkers, you have had experience with strategy. *Strategic planning creates a vision for the future that allows you to anticipate many possibilities and, most importantly, be prepared for them.* Strategic planning is crucial to business success. You can apply the same planning strategy to your life in order to achieve the greatest possible success.

Write a Mission Statement

The first step in strategic planning is to write a mission statement, which will help you stay focused throughout the rest of the planning process. Many businesses and successful people use a mission statement to clarify their goals. It helps them define who they want to be, what they want to do, and what principles are most important to them. Anderson Consulting, one of the largest business consulting firms in the world, stresses the importance of addressing all of these elements:

> You must create a compelling, vivid image of your vision. Paint a picture with your words. Be sure that your soul is in the vision. You or your management cannot apply a vision without it being true. Likewise, your values must come from deep inside. Finally, your mission must be bold, exhilarating, risky, and have a clear finish line.

A mission statement is a statement of intent—a powerful reminder of your most important goals.

To create a mission statement, try to visualize your purpose. What things are most important to you? What values do you want to live by? Create a vivid, bold image of your life's passion and then choose words to describe that picture. Choose words that are descriptive, concise, and stir the imagination of the reader.

Here is author Carol Carter's personal mission statement. You can see that Carol is living an intentional life.

> My mission is to use my talents and abilities to help people of all ages, stages, backgrounds, and economic levels achieve their human potential through fully developing their minds and their talents.

Recent geology graduate, Kristin Groelig, defines her mission in this way:

> To explore and understand the relationships of and interdependencies between the different elements in our natural environment, so that I may educate others and, in the process, help conserve the natural wonders of our country.

Carol's personal mission filters over into the type of work she does, how she interacts with others, and where she volunteers her time. Kristin will work in a different area and use her time in another way, given that her goals will probably be different from Carol's. A mission statement will provide the basis for developing your strategic plan.

You can see from the two different mission statements that being concise is a key component of an effective mission statement. The more narrow or focused your statement, the more it is able to provide you clear guidance for your direction in life. A mission statement is a powerful reminder of your most important goals.

Put Your Goals in Writing

Realizing that your goals may change as you go through the planning process, commit to paper your current short-term and long-term goals, as well as goals from the different areas of your life, such as personal, career, and financial. Make these goals as specific as possible and include a time frame. For example, the geology major, Kristin, has several goals related to her career. One of these goals is to be working in the Department of Natural Resources in Washington, D.C., making national park management decisions for the country by the time she is thirty-five years old.

Analyze Your Strengths and Weaknesses

Strengths and weaknesses are part of who you are and do not relate to the situation that you might be in. Realistically, think about the aspects of yourself that you consider strengths, along with your weaknesses, and list these characteristics. Some of Kristin's strengths include:

- The ability to communicate complicated information in a clear way
- Willingness and ability to adjust to new situations
- A pleasant attitude
- Physical fitness
- Bachelor's degree

Weaknesses are aspects of ourselves that we would like to improve. Some of Kristin's weaknesses include:

- Lack of mathematical and finance knowledge
- Not an independent worker—needs consistent feedback
- Easily frustrated
- Tendency to procrastinate

Analyze the Opportunities and Threats

Opportunities and threats exist in your surroundings and don't have anything to do with your personal characteristics. You can take advantage of the opportunities and work to alleviate the threats. With your goals in mind, think of opportunities and threats that may exist.

For example, in Kristin's case, some of the opportunities she believes exist for her include trends toward:

- Conservation efforts in recent years
- The availability of more financing to fund programs
- Education in elementary public schools on natural resources

Some of the threats she believes exist include the following trends:

- Growing population pressures
- Further forest depletion
- Fewer jobs in forestry management

Reevaluate Your Goals

In light of your analysis so far, what else do you need to do to accomplish your goals? Have you determined any areas that need improvement in order for you to accomplish your objectives? In Kristin's case, by looking at her mission statement, her strengths and weaknesses, and her opportunities and threats, she determined that she wanted to slightly change the identified goal. Factors in her decision included her desire to educate, the fact that fewer people might be needed in land management, and the lack of education in schools. Given this information, she determined that she should concentrate on developing outreach programs, which brings natural resource education to schools. Her goal now is to be the Director of Outreach Programs in the National Park Service by the time she is thirty-five years old. Kristin also realized that she would need to use statistics in this field and would have to develop this skill.

Develop an Action Plan

Your action plan should break your goals down further into manageable pieces. Each of these should have specific measurements, a time line, and resources that are needed. What will you need to do to accomplish your goal? There will be many steps you'll need to follow. For example, part of Kristin's action plan is shown in Figure 2.2.

Figure 2.2 *A sample action plan.*

GOAL	OBJECTIVES	ACTIONS NEEDED	TIME LINE	RESOURCES
1. To become Director of Outreach Programs			January, 2007	
	Work two years in interpretation in a national park and get promoted into next level		January 2001	
		Fill out the federal application	End of next week	Application form
		Interview 10 people currently working in a park	By end of this week	Telephone, Names and numbers of ten employees, List of questions to ask
	Develop math and statistical skills	Register for math class	Next month	School catalogue
	Become more informed of current events in the field	Subscribe to journals	This week	Names and addresses of journals
		Research the Internet	Weekly beginning today	Computer, Internet server
		Go to library	Weekly beginning Monday	Transportation

Implement Your Plan

Once you have made your plan as specific as possible, start working your plan. Though this may sound easy, it is actually the most difficult part of the process. Follow your guidelines and be as true to your timelines as possible. You'll probably find that you'll need to modify the plan as you learn more or run into obstacles, but this should be expected. Developing your strategic plan is meant to be a process that you will change and enhance throughout your life.

Evaluate the Outcome

As you implement your plan, consider what is working and what needs to be changed. Again, this is a tool to use to examine your life and goals and to make your goals become reality. As such, it should be a work-in-progress throughout your career that you will continually evaluate and change.

WHAT TOOLS CAN YOU USE TO ACCOMPLISH WORKPLACE OBJECTIVES?

Goal Setting

Accomplishing workplace goals can be somewhat different from accomplishing the general goals you have for yourself. Although the same basic formula applies—decide what you need to do and set steps for doing it—workplace goals are much more demanding. If you don't buy a car this year, there are few, if any, negative consequences. On the other hand, if you fail to meet the demands of the job, you could quickly be out of work.

Businesses have goals that must be accomplished if the business is to meet its objectives. Although this may sound fairly simple, sometimes the *stated* objectives of an organization and the *actual* objectives can be very different. For instance, if a company says it puts customers first but has a rigid "no returns" policy, its stated objectives are probably different than its actual ones. Again, if a company claims to support family values and at the same time expects employees to travel extensively or put in regular overtime, it may also have values that are different than what is stated.

Managing conflicting workplace objectives. Most businesses have several objectives at any given moment and these objectives can sometimes be conflicting. Imagine a company that has two different departments, both of which need your help to complete their projects by the end of the month. If there is not enough time to do both, how do you decide where to spend your time?

Besides businesses, employees like yourself may also have stated objectives that are entirely different from their actual objectives. For example, a manager may state that the purpose of the impending staff meeting is to discuss salaries but, instead, may really want to spend the meeting talking about project deadlines. This can be unsettling for employees. Imagine how difficult work would be if no one knew what was actually expected. Your responsibility, as an employee, will be to make sure that what others are saying is actually what they want. In addition, you'll need to make sure your own intentions are crystal clear to others. You can do this in the following ways:

Ask for clarification. When your boss hands you an assignment, repeat the expectation. If the project conflicts with a previous assignment, ask which one has priority. If necessary, make a list of your projects and schedule a time to discuss your workload and how to prioritize with your supervisor. If you are doing work for two managers and the goals they have set for you are conflicting, outline the problem to both managers. They should resolve the issue between themselves or with help from their supervisor.

Be clear. When you are giving instructions or assigning projects, be clear about what you want. Ask for feedback so you know that your message was understood.

Confront discrepancies. Even though it may be uncomfortable, effectively addressing workplace ambiguities and discrepancies can be an enormously helpful employee attribute.

Time Management

Time is a resource, just like money, that can be budgeted. Many efficient people arrange their daily schedules according to priorities. Whether you use numbers, letters, colors, or symbols to indicate priorities, your schedule will make more sense and be more effective if you order activities by their importance. The time you spend up front will save you time and frustration in the future.

Managing your time takes consistent thought and planning. Once you understand where you're spending your time and which activities are receiving the most attention, try using the following strategies:

Plan your schedule each week. For each week, note the special events, your goals for the week, and their order of priority. You can put your weekly obligations in a daytimer or on a calendar-at-a-glance. Some people also like to see their goals and schedules by month or year. If you need a more detailed system, use any additional calendars or reminders that work best for you.

Use to-do lists. Many people use to-do lists to help them stay focused on their goals and obligations. Make a list of everything you need to do for the day and prioritize the items. You can use an a, b, c approach, whereby "a" items are urgent, "b" items are important, and "c" items can wait until the others are done. Using to-do lists on a daily basis can make an enormous difference in helping you maintain an organized life. Keep in mind that it is rare for people to accomplish everything on their to-do list in a given day. Do what you can and do what has priority first. Then anything left over can go on the next day's list.

Make thinking about your schedule a priority. The ten or fifteen minutes you give to organizing your schedule can save you hours of time during your week. This way, you'll know what needs to be accomplished ahead of time.

Refer to your schedule. If you don't look at it, it really won't make a significant difference. And more than likely, you'll miss appointments and events that are important to you. Refer to your planner or to-do list frequently throughout the day.

Include unscheduled time and "down" time in your schedule. Don't become so overly scheduled that there's no time for relaxation or spontaneous activities. Everyone needs blocks of time for rest and renewal, and if you don't have these, you won't be as productive. It may seem impractical, but by taking breaks and doing activities, you are actually fueling yourself to get more work done. If you don't schedule the breaks, you will lose just as much worktime, but in a less productive fashion.

Even with the most organized plans and intentions, many people still have difficulty staying on course during their day. The following section addresses procrastination and gives some tips for avoiding traps that eat away at your precious time. How many times have you said to yourself, "I'll take care of that later"? Sometimes you have a good reason to put things off; however, procrastination occurs when you habitually postpone unpleasant or demanding tasks. Procrastination is often deliberate, especially when you are facing something that is challenging or unpleasant. It's easy to find lots of little projects to attend to when you want to avoid something. But the energy you put into avoiding a task might just as well be spent completing the task. Listed here are a few strategies for fighting procrastination.

- Weigh the benefits to you and others of completing the task versus the effects of procrastinating.
- Ask for assistance when you need help with tasks and projects at school, work, and home.
- Be gentle with yourself. Don't expect perfection.
- Talk to yourself positively.
- Establish your time frame for accomplishing the task and then stick to it.
- Get started by breaking the task into simple steps and approaching them one at a time.
- If you have writer's block, start writing the body of a document instead of the beginning.

Strategic Planning

Just as you can complete a plan for yourself, you can also plan for your company, department, or project. Many companies work from a strategic plan, and by referring to your company's mission statement, you will be able to assess the company's priorities. Everything you do while working for the company should be helping, in some way, to achieve that mission.

For example, Rubbermaid's mission statement identifies what the company is about and helps the employees make choices based on what is most important to the company as a whole.

> To be the leading world-class creator and marketer of brand-name, primarily plastic products, which are creatively responsive to global trends and capable of earning a leading market share position.

IN THE REAL WORLD: ILENE BRODY

"My grandfather was a tremendous influence in my life," said Ilene Brody. "He was a wonderful story teller, telling stories about his life, always with themes like 'anything is possible,' and 'anything can be overcome.'"

Ilene has embraced her grandfather's philosophy all of her life. Her grandfather came from a very poor background, and he succeeded by utilizing ingenuity and persistence. Ilene has patterned her own life in the same way. As vice president of Network Operations at US West Communications, the highest position in her company held by a woman, she has proven that, indeed, anything is possible if the will to succeed exists.

Her grandfather's example provided Ilene with a solid foundation that gave her the motivation to succeed. Following high school, she proceeded directly to college, and continued on through graduate school, earning her Ph.D. in psychology from Columbia University.

Ilene put her schooling and analytical skills to work, developing a system of problem solving that evolved into an entire curriculum still practiced in the New Jersey school system. The program not only encourages development of problem-solving skills, but independent thought as well. Ilene's purpose was to encourage children to explore the possibilities in life. "I enjoy giving people the capability to go to their next step. I want people to ask questions and realize that they have the capabilities to come away with solutions."

After finishing her doctoral dissertation, Ilene was able to put her ideas to work successfully in companies around the country. As a consultant, she has reorganized the workings of factories and entire companies to provide a more comfortable and supportive atmosphere. She locates problems and works with the employees to reach solutions. She then teaches employees how they can work through challenges by asking the proper questions, which leads to making decisions that are acceptable to all parties. This also creates a positive atmosphere within a company, allowing employees to reach their full productive potential.

Now employed by one of the largest communications companies in the United States, Ilene acknowledges that it hasn't always been easy. She's seen the glass ceiling and dealt with organizations that favored the traditional idea of all-male management. As a single mother, she has encountered moments when her responsibilities as an employee conflicted with her responsibilities as a parent—"There have been times when it has been really lonely." Sometimes success has a price, but Ilene asserts that attitude determines your ability to rise above it. Her own positive outlook keeps her confident in her ability to take on new challenges successfully.

According to Ilene, the ability to analyze and seek out solutions is a primary factor in determining success. Additionally, she suggests that one should be able to view issues in a diversified manner and possess the drive to take occasional risks. A strong sense of self, the ability to think beyond the here and now, and a positive attitude are necessary components for a successful and well-rounded person. Ilene herself exemplifies these qualities. A successful mother and professional, Ilene's story is an encouragement not only to those who strive to find a balance between their personal and professional lives, but also for those who have dreams to pursue. In the words of her grandfather, "Anything is possible."

SUMMARY

Successful people spend time defining goals, planning ways to accomplish those goals, and taking action.

Your goals, your basic values, your enduring purpose, and your mission are all components of the general vision you have for your career and for your life, and a strategic plan can help to keep you focused. You can set short-term and long-term goals or set them by areas of your life, including personal, career, and financial. Sometimes you'll find that you have conflicting goals, in which case you can brainstorm solutions, evaluate the solutions, and determine which one is best for your situation.

A strategic plan, which can help you organize and fulfill your goals, begins with setting a mission statement for yourself. Accomplishing workplace goals can be somewhat different from accomplishing the general goals you have for yourself, but it is made easier by setting the goals in writing, managing conflicting workplace objectives, managing your time, and using strategic planning.

Chapter 2 Bringing Your Dreams to Reality

2.1 Time Management

To determine how much of your time is given to a single goal in an individual day, you'll need to keep a daily log. For the next week, analyze how much time you spend on your main activities (use the form provided). Make sure your totals equal 24 hours for a day. When you're finished, you'll chart your hours to give you a visual representation of how you spend your time. Then you'll assess whether the time you're giving is going in the direction of the things you value most.

	MON	TUE	WED	THU	FRI	SAT	SUN	TOTAL
Sleep								24
School								24
Work								24
Homework								24
Family/ Chores								24
Travel/ Commute								24
Entertainment								24
Exercise								24

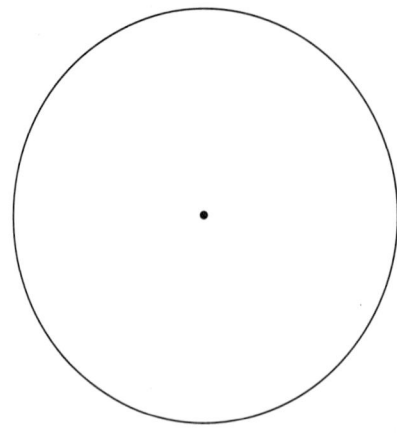

Next, chart the total hours spent on each activity in the circle. Use different colored pens or pencils to differentiate the different activities. Which activity receives the most amount of your time? The least? Is the way you divide your time acceptable? Why or why not?

On a separate piece of paper, do the same thing for your work schedule. (If you're not working at this time, team up with someone who is and do the project together or interview someone on staff at your school.) Note how much time is devoted to the following:

Lunch breaks	Writing memos	Solving problems
Coffee breaks	Planning your day	Developing plans
Staff meetings	Organizing materials/filing	Actual work
Personal conversations	Mentoring others	

When you are finished, share your charts with the rest of the class. What are the similarities? What receives the majority of your daily attention? What needs to change so that you are more effective?

 Making a To-Do List

Make a to-do list for everything you have to do tomorrow. Generally, you should include all tasks and events, regular activities, and activities you'd like to do if there's time. When you are finished, rank the tasks or events according to whether they are high priorities, regular ones, or ones that can possibly be put off to another day. Use the list on the following day and observe whether it helped you accomplish your tasks more effectively.

 How Do You Procrastinate?

1. Name up to three habitual excuses that you (or people you know) use to avoid something you (they) don't want to do.

   _____
   _____
   _____
   _____

2. What are the effects of procrastination? Check the sentences that apply and add some of your own.

   _____ It affects your grades.

   _____ You're not as productive.

   _____ Your work suffers.

   _____ You feel bad about yourself.

   _____ You arrive late to important functions.

   _____ Friends get angry or feel let down by your behavior.

   _____ Your stress levels increase.

   _____ You end up having to work late or on weekends to make up for your procrastination.

   _____ Other: _____
   _____
   _____

3. Think about a specific time you procrastinated. What happened?
___
___
___

4. Work on changing one of your procrastination habits. What steps will you take?
___
___
___

5. List three benefits of starting projects early or on time.
___
___
___

2.4 Goal Setting

Write a long-term career goal in the space provided.

Goal: _____
___

Now think about some of the steps involved in accomplishing your goal. The steps might be making phone calls or appointments or filling out applications. The step could even be as complex as completing your education. List the steps below. When you are finished, look back over your list and decide what step comes first, second, and so on. Put the corresponding number next to the step. Then try the whole process once more.

STEPS:	RANK
___	___
___	___
___	___
___	___

Goal: _____

STEPS:	RANK
___	___
___	___
___	___
___	___

PERSONAL ASSETS

Your Mission...

Using the mission statement examples from the chapter as a guide, create your own mission statement. Begin by choosing five mental images that illustrate what you want out of life and what is most meaningful to you. Use these images as a way to draft your mission statement. For example, you may see yourself as a whirlwind of energy exuding dynamic potential as you propel yourself across new horizons. You may see yourself as a quiet stream, gently moving in the direction of your dreams while giving life to the plants and animals around you. Once you have created your five images, take the words that most express your mission and form your mission statement. For example, after drawing from the two previous images you might say . . .

My mission is to use my dynamic energy to feed the hungry of the world.

Use the form below to enter your five images. When you are finished, write your mission statement in the space provided. You may want to use an extra piece of paper for your first draft.

1. _____
2. _____
3. _____
4. _____
5. _____

YOUR MISSION

_____
_____
_____
_____
_____

WORKING TOGETHER

Comparing Priorities

Just like the two students who compared their priorities earlier in the chapter, now is your chance to compare your priorities to those of other students in your class. In groups of three to five, begin by brainstorming a list of long-term goals. Have one member of the group keep a record. From that list, pick out ten goals

to which everyone can relate. Each group member should then take five minutes alone to rank the goals according to his or her personal priority. Use a 1 to 10 scale, with 1 being the most important and 10 having the lowest priority.

When everyone is finished, examine the rankings of each group member. Discuss why the orders are different or similar. What makes one person rank something high while another person ranks it low? If there is time, have the group circle the items that received the same ranking throughout the group (if there are any). Return to the large group and discuss your findings with the other class members.

CASE STUDIES

What Would You Do?

John was an organizational development consultant with only a few months on the job. His first assignment was to assess the communication effectiveness and general levels of satisfaction in a public utilities company. John began by holding individual meetings with the employees. After that, he met privately with every upper and middle manager. Even though it took several weeks, John felt he clearly understood both the problems and strengths of the company. He developed his final report noting specific steps the company could take and made arrangements to present his findings to the executives. John's report noted that

1. *Employee expectations were not clearly stated*
2. *Employees did not feel that they received enough feedback*
3. *Morale was low due to the imprecise goals*
4. *Managers did not have consistent practices*

Gather into small groups and discuss the following items. Make notes in the space provided.

- What are the main problems?

- What steps should the managers take to handle the situation?

CHAPTER 2   BRINGING YOUR DREAMS TO REALITY   **37**

- How can they effectively alleviate the problems?

- What methods of feedback can they use?

- What are some effective methods for raising morale?

When you are finished, present your ideas to the rest of the class.

Jennifer has just received her six-month performance review. She is disappointed that her overall performance rating was average, with some deficiencies noted, for example, attention to detail and timely completion of work. Jennifer takes pride in getting her work done and doesn't understand her supervisor's remarks. He said she'd have to do more than the minimum if she wants a better rating. Jennifer doesn't understand why getting the work done isn't good enough.

Identify the problems Jennifer is facing. Discuss the steps you would take to alleviate or minimize the situation if you found yourself in similar circumstances. Look at the six-month time frame. Could anything have been done earlier by Jennifer or her boss before the review?

- Does she understand the requirements for success?

- What are the issues that caused Jennifer to receive an average rating?

- What habits may have been developed by Jennifer in school that are limiting her performance in her career now?

- What suggestions might you give Jennifer?

- Should Jennifer let her boss know the steps she intends to take to correct the problem? If so, how should she approach the discussion?

Learning Styles

How to Become a Lifelong Learner

KEY CONCEPTS

- What is your learning style?
- How can understanding your learning style help you become more effective and efficient on the job?

> What sculpture is to a block of marble, education is to a human soul.
>
> Joseph Addison

In today's world of intensifying competition, rapid technological innovation, and an increasingly diverse population, learning is not an option at work—it is crucial to your success. As technology advances and the body of knowledge in your field grows, you will need to keep informed of changes to sustain your value. Although it is impossible to learn today everything you will need to know in the future, you can learn how to be an effective learner throughout your career.

There is no one best way to learn. Instead, there are several different learning styles that are suited to different situations. The goal of this chapter is to help you become aware of your most effective learning styles. Knowing how you take in and process information can save you countless hours of attempting to gather information using ineffective methods. Each individual will use these learning styles in a different combination, many times relying on one or two dominant styles. Once you understand your unique learning style combination, you will accomplish the following:

- Process information more quickly
- Retain what you learn
- Know what kind of work environment best suits your style
- Know how to relate to learning styles that are different from your own

"All the men in my family work with their hands designing jewelry," says Leo Di Angelo. "After I completed high school, it was assumed that I would continue in the family tradition and enter the family-run jewelry design center. The problem was that I just couldn't generate any enthusiasm for my future. The thought of designing jewelry and then creating it from scratch seemed overwhelming. What I really liked was interacting with people—especially young people. I had volunteered at the central community center every summer as the baseball coach and discovered I had a real talent for working with kids. Even though I knew my family would probably freak, I talked to my counselor at the school and got information about getting my teaching certification.

It was pretty hard on my father to let go of his dream for me, but thankfully, he did. I have since gone on to graduate with honors with a degree in teaching. I began working just last year. During my time in school I discovered how important it is to learn about the different types of ways people learn. The information hit me like a ton of bricks. It was at this point that I realized that I learn differently than other members of my family learn. While most of them are happy working with their hands and can visualize designs with ease, I function best when I can verbalize and express. Teaching to them would be a painful ordeal, whereas for me, it is an absolute joy."

WHAT IS YOUR LEARNING STYLE?

Educational psychologists have worked diligently at categorizing learning styles according to how people gather information. This is no easy task because we are all truly unique individuals with complex thinking systems. The simplest method is to categorize learning styles by how we intake information through our senses. The different senses are listed below.

Hearing (or auditory)
Sight (or visual)
Smell (or olfactory)
Touch (or tactile)
Taste (or gustatory)
Movement (or kinesthetic)
Intuition

Almost everyone gathers information—to some degree—using all of these senses. The degree to which your particular senses are developed affects how well you receive information. For instance, if you learn better when you can see what is being taught, you may learn more easily when there are overhead illustrations or outlines to follow. On the other hand, if you learn best when you can touch, you may have an easier time learning material that is lab-oriented or hands-on. Learning is easier when you have variety of well-developed senses at your disposal.

People also have a preference for either their right brain or their left brain. This is called cognitive preference. Basically the term refers to the way the brain classifies information. Most individuals have a dominant cognitive preference. By recognizing your preference, you can use both sides of your brain more effectively. Understanding the way you take in information and process it once it's been gathered lets you know what you need in a learning environment, and even on the job. You can do the following:

- Learn to develop creative thinking skills
- Learn to use your logical, linear brain
- Make more informed choices through critical thinking
- Recognize other people's cognitive preferences and adjust your style accordingly

What Is Your Cognitive Preference?

The exercise "Personality Spectrum," below, will help you discover your cognitive preference (the side of your brain that you prefer to use when you are processing information).

Your personality spectrum assessment can help you to maximize your functioning at work. Each personality has its own abilities that improve work performance, suitable learning techniques, and ways of relating in interpersonal relationships. Table 3.1 explains which strengths are typical of each personality type.

Another way to discuss how the brain functions is to refer to intelligence. We all know individuals who have demonstrated their ability to understand and remember information, which resulted in excellent grades in their years of formal training. Yet, some of these people have difficulties in coping with day-to-day functions or minor challenges.

PERSONALITY SPECTRUM

Step 1: Rank all four responses to each question from most like you (4), to least like you (1). Place a 1, 2, 3, or 4 in each box next to the responses, and use each number only once per question.

1. I like instructors who
   - [2] a. tell me exactly what is expected of me.
   - [3] b. make learning active and exciting.
   - [1] c. maintain a safe and supportive classroom.
   - [4] d. challenge me to think at higher levels.

2. I learn best when material is
   - [2] a. well organized.
   - [4] b. something I can do hands-on.
   - [1] c. about understanding and improving the human condition.
   - [3] d. intellectually challenging.

3. A high priority in my life is to
   - [2] a. keep my commitments.
   - [3] b. experience as much of life as possible.
   - [1] c. make a difference in other's lives.
   - [4] d. understand how things work.

4. Other people think of me as
   - [3] a. dependable and loyal.
   - [2] b. dynamic and creative.
   - [1] c. caring and honest.
   - [4] d. intelligent and inventive.

5. When I experience stress, I most likely
   - [2] a. do something to help me feel more in control.
   - [3] b. do something physical and daring.
   - [1] c. talk with a friend.
   - [4] d. go off by myself and think about my situation.

6. The greatest flaw someone can have is to be
   - [1] a. irresponsible.
   - [4] b. unwilling to try new things.
   - [2] c. selfish and unkind to others.
   - [3] d. an illogical thinker.

7. My vacations could best be described as
   - [4] a. traditional.
   - [1] b. adventuresome.
   - [2] c. pleasing to others.
   - [3] d. a new learning experience.

8. One word that best describes me is
   - [4] a. sensible.
   - [2] b. spontaneous.
   - [1] c. giving.
   - [3] d. analytical.

Step 2: Add up the total points for each column.

Total Column (A)	Total Column (B)	Total Column (C)	Total Column (D)
20	22	10	28
Organizer	Adventurer	Giver	Thinker

Step 3: Plot these numbers on the brain diagram on the following page.

From *Keys to Success: How to Achieve Your Goals*, 2/e by Carter et al., © 1998. Reprinted by permission of Prentice-Hall, Inc., Upper Saddle River, NJ.

CHAPTER 3 LEARNING STYLES

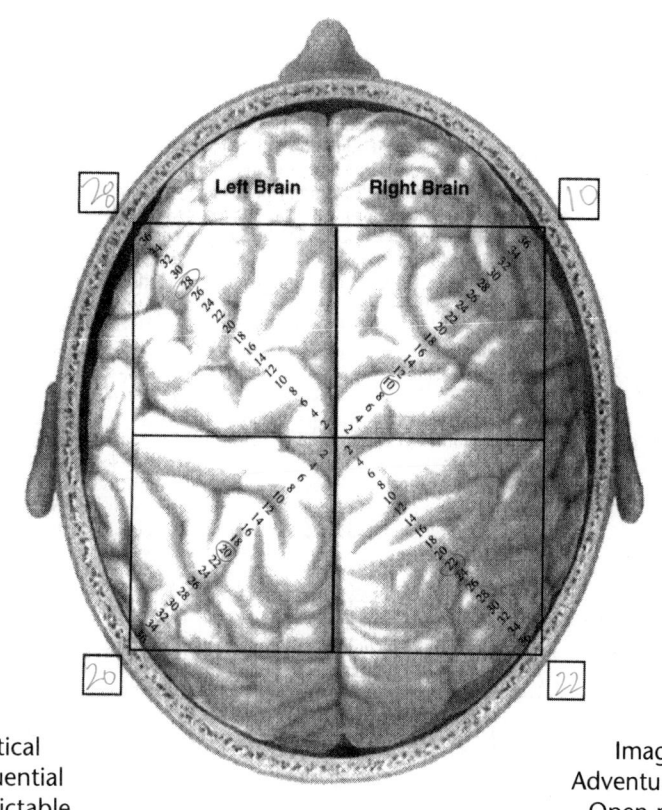

THINKER
Technical
Scientific
Mathematical
Dispassionate
Rational
Analytical
Logical
Problem Solving
Theoretical
Intellectual
Objective
Quantitative
Explicit
Realistic
Literal
Precise
Formal

GIVER
Interpersonal
Emotional
Caring
Sociable
Giving
Spiritual
Musical
Romantic
Feeling
Peacemaker
Trusting
Adaptable
Passionate
Harmonious
Idealistic
Talkative
Honest

ORGANIZER
Systematic
Administrative
Procedural
Organized
Conservative
Confident
Structured
Safekeeping
Disciplined
Practical
Sequential
Predictable
Detailed
Tactical
Controlled
Dependable
Planning

ADVENTURER
Imaginative
Adventuresome
Open-minded
Fast-paced
Metaphoric
Original
Simultaneous
Visual
Impulsive
Experimental
Risking
Divergent
Artistic
Spatial
Skillful
Competitive
Active

From *Keys to Success: How to Achieve Your Goals*, 2/e by Carter et al., © 1998. Reprinted by permission of Prentice-Hall, Inc., Upper Saddle River, NJ.

Table 3.1 *Personality spectrum at work.*

PERSONALITY TYPE	STRENGTHS AT WORK	INTERPERSONAL RELATIONSHIPS
ORGANIZER	Efficient manager of heavy work loads Good organizational skills Natural leadership qualities	Loyal Dependable Traditional
ADVENTURER	Adaptable to most changes Creative and skillful Dynamic and fast-paced	Free Exciting Intense
GIVER	Always willing to help others Honest and sincere Good people skills	Giving Romantic Warm
THINKER	Good analytical skills Thorough and exact Can develop complex designs	Quiet Inventive Good problem solver

The movie *Shine*, for example, portrayed the life of a man who could passionately understand and bring to life exceptionally beautiful piano concertos yet was unable to effectively communicate with others. His brain processed information in such a way that, on the one hand, he was able to perform at extremely high levels of competence, while on the other hand, he needed special care to function normally.

Howard Gardner, a research psychologist, believes there are at least eight distinct intelligences possessed by all people and that people develop some intelligences more fully than others. According to his theory, when you learn something easily, you are probably using an intelligence that is fully developed. If you have difficulty learning a particular type of information, you are probably using a less developed intelligence. Table 3.2 describes these eight forms of intelligence.

Table 3.2 *Multiple intelligences.*

INTELLIGENCE	DEFINITION
Verbal–Linguistic	Ability to communicate through language (listening, writing, speaking)
Logical–Mathematical	Ability to understand logical reasoning and problem solving (math, science, patterns, sequences)
Bodily–Kinesthetic	Ability to use the physical body skillfully and to take in knowledge through bodily sensations (coordination, working with hands)
Visual–Spatial	Ability to understand spatial relationships and to perceive and create images (visual arts, graphic design, charts, maps)
Interpersonal Intelligence	Ability to relate to others, noticing their moods, motivations, and feelings (social activity, cooperative learning, teamwork)
Intrapersonal Intelligence	Ability to understand one's own behavior and feelings (time spent alone, independence)
Musical Intelligence	Ability to comprehend and create meaningful sound (music, sensitivity to sound)
Naturalistic Intelligence	Ability to understand features of the environment (interest in nature, environmental balance, ecosystem, stress relief brought by natural environments)

Please complete the following assessment of your multiple intelligences, called "Pathways to Learning," developed by Joyce Bishop. It will help you determine which of your intelligences are most fully developed. Don't be concerned if some of your scores are low. That is true of most people, even your instructors and your authors!

Learning styles and multiple intelligences are gauges to help you understand yourself. After completing the assessments, you may find that you have an increased awareness of your learning styles and how you can use this information to maximize your learning.

PATHWAYS TO LEARNING

Directions: Rate each statement as follows: rarely 1; sometimes 2; usually 3; always 4.
Write the number of your response (1–4) in the box next to the statement and total each set of the six questions.

Developed by Joyce Bishop and based upon Howard Gardner, *Frames of Mind: The Theory of Multiple Intelligences.*

- [4] 1. I enjoy physical activities.
- [4] 2. I am uncomfortable sitting still.
- [4] 3. I prefer to learn through doing.
- [4] 4. When sitting I move my legs or hands.
- [4] 5. I enjoy working with my hands.
- [2] 6. I like to pace when I'm thinking or studying.
- [22] **TOTAL for Bodily–Kinesthetic**

- [ ] 7. I use maps easily.
- [ ] 8. I draw pictures/diagrams when explaining ideas.
- [ ] 9. I can assemble items easily from diagrams.
- [ ] 10. I enjoy drawing or photography.
- [ ] 11. I do not like to read long paragraphs.
- [ ] 12. I prefer a drawn map over written directions.
- [ ] **TOTAL for Visual–Spatial**

- [ ] 13. I enjoy telling stories.
- [ ] 14. I like to write.
- [ ] 15. I like to read.
- [ ] 16. I express myself clearly.
- [ ] 17. I am good at negotiating.
- [ ] 18. I like to discuss topics that interest me.
- [ ] **TOTAL for Verbal–Linguistic**

- [ ] 19. I like math in school.
- [ ] 20. I like science.
- [ ] 21. I problem-solve well.
- [ ] 22. I question how things work.
- [ ] 23. I enjoy planning or designing something new.
- [ ] 24. I am able to fix things.
- [ ] **TOTAL for Logical–Mathematical**

- [ ] 25. I listen to music.
- [ ] 26. I move my fingers or feet when I hear music.
- [ ] 27. I have good rhythm.
- [ ] 28. I like to sing along with music.
- [ ] 29. People have said I have musical talent.
- [ ] 30. I like to express my ideas through music.
- [ ] **TOTAL for Musical**

- [ ] 31. I like doing a project with other people.
- [ ] 32. People come to me to help settle conflicts.
- [ ] 33. I like to spend time with friends.
- [ ] 34. I am good at understanding people.
- [ ] 35. I am good at making people feel comfortable.
- [ ] 36. I enjoy helping others.
- [ ] **TOTAL for Interpersonal**

- [ ] 37. I need quiet time to think.
- [ ] 38. I think about issues before I want to talk.
- [ ] 39. I am interested in self-improvement.
- [ ] 40. I understand my thoughts and feelings.
- [ ] 41. I know what I want out of life.
- [ ] 42. I prefer to work on projects alone.
- [ ] **TOTAL for Intrapersonal**

- [ ] 43. I enjoy nature whenever possible.
- [ ] 44. I think about having a career involving nature.
- [ ] 45. I enjoy studying plants, animals, or oceans.
- [ ] 46. I avoid being indoors except when I sleep.
- [ ] 47. As a child I played with bugs and leaves.
- [ ] 48. When I feel stressed I want to be out in nature.
- [ ] **TOTAL for Naturalistic**

Write each of your eight intelligences in the column where it fits below. For each, choose the column that corresponds with your total in that intelligence.

Scores of 20–24 Highly Developed		Scores of 14–19 Moderately Developed		Scores below 14 Underdeveloped	
Scores	Intelligences	Scores	Intelligences	Scores	Intelligences
	Bodily-Kinesthetic Visual-Spatial Logical-Mathematical Intrapersonal		Musical Interpersonal Naturalistic		Verbal-Linguistic

Keys to Success, 2/e by Carter et al., 1998. Reprinted by permission of Prentice-Hall, Inc., Upper Saddle River, NJ.

HOW CAN UNDERSTANDING YOUR LEARNING STYLE HELP YOU BECOME MORE EFFECTIVE AND EFFICIENT?

Knowing your learning style and the styles of those with whom you work can help increase your effectiveness on the job in many ways. By understanding how you best learn, you will be able to more easily remember important information, critically assess new information, and understand your coworkers, which will help in conflict resolution.

Although businesses have traditionally favored verbal–linguistic learners, there is no general benefit to one style over another. The key advantage to knowing your learning style is that it will help you know how you absorb and process information. Following are additional benefits of knowing your learning styles.

Knowing How You Learn and How You Relate to the World Will Help You Make Smarter Choices

By understanding your learning style, you can choose the type of work and work situation that supports your dominant style. You will also be prepared for situations that use the other styles and adjust to these situations accordingly.

IN THE REAL WORLD: DICK BOUDREAU

Dick Boudreau remembers his introduction to the banking industry with a touch of humor.

> When my aunt suggested that I apply to the bank for a job, I was fresh out of high school and looking to earn a few dollars. She told me in a matter-of-fact way to go right down to the bank and ask for a job. Of course, they would give it to me, she reasoned—I was her nephew. It worked. I got the job and became a bank teller.

Dick worked for a year and a half until he was drafted into the U.S. Navy. In the military, he found that he quickly matured.

> The military expects you to grow up right away. I found that I had more responsibility than in civilian life, which was good because it pushed me to work towards advancement. I feel that I emerged from my time in the Navy with the desire to push forward; to always keep advancing.

Dick feels that success starts with an inner drive to succeed. He believes that one should keep setting goals and, upon reaching them, set more. Once he completed his military service, he returned home. He felt driven and knew that he wanted to attend school. Through the use of the GI Bill, Dick was able to attend college on a part-time basis, eventually earning an associate's degree in business. Working full-time at the bank had given him his entrance into the financial world.

> A college education is not nearly the same thing now as it was then. There is no possible way that young people will be able to advance unless they have a good education. Where the simple drive to succeed worked favorably for me, a young person now needs a good education to support that drive.

Dick worked at the bank in several capacities, but he knew that he had really accomplished something significant when he reached what had previously been a long-shot goal. He was made vice-president and regional manager over four other branches. His persistence and drive paid off for him. Dick's philosophy on life is simple:

> I always try to put myself in the other person's place when dealing with people. I think about how I would want someone to deal with me. Beyond that, I try to refrain from interfering in the affairs of others. It's really a very simple philosophy—'Do unto others as you would have them do unto you'—it works every time.

Although he has enjoyed success professionally, Dick feels that he has been truly successful personally as well. "My primary motivator now is my wife—she keeps me going." Dick has also seen to it that his three children received their college education. Dick also thinks that a positive attitude is of utmost importance, as it determines others' perceptions of you.

> Have a positive attitude and take your life seriously—remember, there's nothing that you can't do if you set your mind to it.

You Can Be More Successful on the Job

Your learning style is essential to your working style. If you find yourself nodding off during oral presentations, and you are a visual learner, you may need to track the flow of information with diagrams. If you learn and work best in group settings, find work situations that support team work.

You Can Become Better at Pinpointing Areas in Which You Need Improvement

Knowing your learning style can help you identify your own strengths and weaknesses as well as the strengths and weaknesses of others. Watch how others in your immediate work area process information. Can you identify their learning styles? If so, you'll understand how to address them with the information you want them to have. Think about whether they could benefit from receiving written information. Would verbalizing your message work as well? Learn to identify others' learning styles, and it will help you understand how to interact with your peers and supervisors.

You Can Put Multiple Intelligences to Work

By understanding how you learn best, and by using your dominant intelligences and learning styles, you can maximize your effectiveness at work. The following selection is a sample of suggestions that working people with one dominant intelligence have given for increasing productivity.

Visual–spatial intelligence. If you are dominant in this intelligence, you could try using the following suggestions at work:

- Add diagrams to your notes whenever possible.
- Draw project deadlines on a time line.
- Graph math functions.
- Show percentages on a pie chart.
- Connect related facts with arrows.
- Color code your notes and to-do lists with highlighters.
- When giving presentations, use visual aids, such as overhead transparencies, Microsoft PowerPoint, or charts, to illustrate your point.

Verbal–linguistic intelligence. If you are dominant in this intelligence, try using these ideas:

- Explain ideas and concepts to others.
- Read work materials aloud.
- Repeat back information your coworkers or boss give you.
- Summarize the results of your meetings aloud.

Bodily–kinesthetic intelligence. To maximize your learning ability if your dominant intelligence is body-kinesthetic, try using the following suggestions:

- Apply the information to real-world examples.
- Relate learning to personal experience.
- Make up poems or songs about the information.
- Role play.
- Use flash cards.
- Review material while walking.
- Move around when you are speaking.

Intrapersonal intelligence. If you are more reflective, and work best when alone, or when independent, you may want to try the following ideas:

- Work in a quiet area.
- Let coworkers know you'll get back to them after you've had a chance to think things through.
- Keep a note pad handy so you can jot down ideas you've had during the day or evening hours.
- Use your quiet time, lunch, exercise time, or commute to reflect on work.

Logical–mathematical intelligence. If you are adept at understanding logical reasoning and problem solving, you could use the following suggestions at work:

- Use your style in business meetings to help others stay on task.
- Prepare for meetings by writing out your personal agenda. Have copies of your materials available for others, so that they may follow your agenda.
- When people jump from topic to topic, keep track of the information by using diagrams or think links.

JOBS AND LEARNING STYLES

Review the Personality Spectrum exercise you completed earlier in this chapter. Were you an organizer, giver, adventurer, or thinker? Why should your personality determine the type of work you should do? If you were an adventurer at heart, you might find it difficult to sit at a computer crunching numbers for the rest of your career. However, if you are an organizer or thinker, this type of job might sound ideal to you.

Some jobs found to go well with different learning styles are listed below, but don't be limited by these. You can really do anything you want to do, and there are literally hundreds of thousands of options available. If you can fit your personality style to your work, the goals you pursue will likely be easier to attain, and you'll have more fun in the process.

In the list below, fill in other types of work that might fit each personality type.

ORGANIZER

Strategic Planner, Buyer, Graphic Designer, Event Coordinator, Fund Raiser

_____
_____
_____
_____
_____

GIVER

Nurse, Pastor, Teacher, Counselor, Lawyer, Social Worker, Veterinarian, Attorney, Mechanic, Financial Consultant

_____
_____
_____
_____
_____

ADVENTURER

Entrepreneur, Pilot, Travel Agent, Sales, Radio and News Personality, Writer, Police Officer

_____
_____
_____
_____

THINKER

Scientist, Researcher, Computer Programmer, Banker, Editor, Lawyer, Accountant

_____
_____
_____
_____
_____

SUMMARY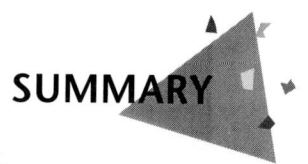

*Let your learning style enhance your success.
Maximize your learning style strengths
and effectively manage your learning style limitations.*

Knowing your particular learning style can help you find success on the job and in your life. You'll have a much easier time if you understand the type of thinker you are and can apply your style to make contributions in the work force. And if you take the time to understand the learning styles of other employees with whom you work, you'll have working relationships that are much more effective.

Your personality, and how it fits with your career choice, can also affect your success in the workplace. Knowing how you learn, what best suits your personality, and how you relate to the world will help you make smarter choices and pinpoint areas in which you need improvement. Considering your learning styles when choosing a career could give you an advantage in reaching your goals.

Application & Exercises

PERSONAL ASSETS

Learning Styles Inventory

The following inventory can help you discover more information about how you learn and process information. When you are finished, review the information on multiple intelligences to gain a deeper insight into your style.

Please complete the inventory below by circling **a** or **b** to indicate your answer to each question. Answer every question and choose only one answer for each question. If both answers seem to apply to you, choose the answer that applies most often.

From *Keys to Success: How to Achieve Your Goals,* 2/e by Carter et al., © 1998. Reprinted by permission of Prentice-Hall, Inc., Upper Saddle River, NJ.

1. I study best
   a. in a study group.
   b. alone or with a partner.

2. I would rather be considered
   a. realistic.
   b. imaginative.

3. When I recall what I did yesterday, I am most likely to think in terms of
   a. pictures/images.
   b. words/verbal descriptions.

4. I usually think new material is
   a. easier at the beginning and then harder as it gets more complicated.
   b. harder at the beginning but easier as I begin to understand what the whole subject is about.

5. When given a new activity to learn, I would rather first
   a. try it out.
   b. think about how I'm going to do it.

6. If I were an instructor, I would rather teach a course that deals with
   a. real-life situations and what to do about them.
   b. ideas and encourage students to think about them.

7. I prefer to receive new information in the form of
   a. pictures, diagrams, graphs, or maps.
   b. written information or verbal instructions.

8. I learn
   a. at a fairly regular pace. If I study hard I'll "get it" and then move on.
   b. in fits and starts. I might be totally confused and then it all "clicks."

9. I understand something better after I
   a. attempt to do it myself.
   b. give myself time to think about how it works.

10. I find it easier to
    a. learn facts.
    b. learn ideas/concepts.

11. In a book with lots of pictures and charts, I am likely to
    a. look over the pictures and charts carefully.
    b. focus on the written text.

12. It's easier for me to memorize facts from
    a. a list.
    b. a whole story/essay with the facts embedded in the text.

13. I will more easily remember
    a. something I have done myself.
    b. something I have thought or read about.

14. I am usually
    a. aware of my surroundings. I remember people and places and am able to easily find things I have set aside.
    b. unaware of my surroundings. I usually forget people and places and frequently misplace things.

15. I like instructors
    a. who put a lot of diagrams on the board.
    b. who spend a lot of time explaining.

16. Once I understand
    a. all the parts, I understand the whole thing.
    b. the whole thing, I see how the parts fit.

17. When I am learning something new, I would rather
    a. talk about it.
    b. think about it.

18. I am good at
    a. being careful about the details of my work.
    b. having creative ideas about how to do my work.

19. I remember best
    a. what I see.
    b. what I hear.

20. When I solve problems that involve math, I usually
    a. work my way to the solution one step at a time.
    b. see the solutions but then struggle to figure out the steps to get to them.

21. In a lecture class, I would prefer occasionally in-class
    a. discussions or group problem-solving sessions.
    b. pauses that give opportunities to think or write about ideas presented in the lecture.

22. On a multiple-choice test, I am more likely to
    a. run out of time.
    b. lose points because of not reading carefully or making careless mistakes.

23. When I get a direction to a new place, I prefer
    a. a map.
    b. written instructions.

24. When I'm thinking about something I've read
    a. I remember the incidents and try to put them together to create a theme.
    b. I just know what the themes are when I finish reading.

25. When I get a new VCR or computer, I tend to
    a. plug it in and start punching buttons.
    b. read the manual and follow directions.

26. In reading for pleasure, I prefer
    a. something that teaches me new facts or tells me how to do something.
    b. something that gives me new ideas to think about.

27. When I see a diagram or sketch in class, I am most likely to remember
    a. the picture.
    b. what the instructor said about it.

28. It is more important to me that the instructor
    a. lay out the material in clear, sequential steps.
    b. give me an overall picture and relate the material to other subjects.

54 CHAPTER 3 LEARNING STYLES

LEARNING STYLES INVENTORY SCORES

1. Put a numeral 1 in the appropriate boxes in the table; for example, if you answered **a** to question number 3, put a 1 in the column headed **a** next to the number 3. If you answered **b** to question 4, put a numeral 1 in the **b** column next to number 4.
2. Total the 1s in the columns and write the totals in the indicated spaces at the base of the columns.

Write totals for each column in the spaces below.

ACTIVE/REFLECTIVE			FACTUAL/THEORETICAL			VISUAL/VERBAL			LINEAR/HOLISTIC		
Q#	a	b	Q#	a	b	Q#	a	b	Q#	a	b
1			2			3			4		
5			6			7			8		
9			10			11			12		
13			14			15			16		
17			18			19			20		
21			22			23			24		
25			26			27			28		
Total			Total			Total			Total		

3.1 How Do You Learn Best?

Write the scores you calculated throughout the chapter in the spaces below.

LEARNING STYLES INVENTORY	PATHWAYS TO LEARNING	PERSONALITY SPECTRUM
_____ Active	_____ Bodily–Kinesthetic	_____ Organizer
_____ Reflective	_____ Visual–Spatial	_____ Adventurer
_____ Factual	_____ Verbal–Linguistic	_____ Giver
_____ Theoretical	_____ Logical–Mathematical	_____ Thinker
_____ Visual	_____ Musical	
_____ Verbal	_____ Interpersonal	
_____ Linear	_____ Intrapersonal	
_____ Holistic	_____ Naturalist	

WORKING TOGETHER

Comparing Learning Styles

By now, all of you should have a relatively good understanding of your learning style—its strengths and limitations. Once you have divided into your small groups (3–5 people), have everyone share his or her learning style with the rest of the group. Discuss what types of learning situations are difficult for you and what types of learning situations are easy. Think about a job you have now or one you've had in the past. Was the job supportive of your learning style or did you struggle matching your style against the needs of the employer and the company expectations? Share your experience.

When the groups are finished discussing, divide into new groups according to your dominant learning style (all sequential learners together, all reflective learners together etc.). Discuss the same things you did in the last group. This time, though, observe how much you have in common with the others. Answer the following questions about your two group meetings:

1. What did you discover about the different learning styles of the first group?

2. Which style would you prefer to have if you could change? Why?

3. Which style is the most difficult for you to interact with? Why?

4. What can you do to increase your effectiveness with your least favorite style?

5. What one thing would you like others to know about how you learn best?

CASE STUDIES

One

WHAT WOULD YOU DO?

Nyland has always been shy. In college his professors frequently commented on his reluctance to participate in class discussions. Now that Nyland is employed full-time, he's finding that his inability to dialogue is hampering his effectiveness on the job. He dreads the weekly staff meeting because he must give a formal report on his department's performance. Nyland knows that if he doesn't change soon his chance of advancement is slim to none. What can he do?

Gather into pairs and discuss steps Nyland can take to change or compensate for his behavior.

- List the steps you recommend. _____

- Which learning style(s) is probably dominant? _____

- Least developed? _____

Critical and Creative Thinking

4

Expanding Your Mind

KEY CONCEPTS

- How can you use critical thinking skills to solve problems?
- How can you use creative thinking to make better decisions?
- What is emotional intelligence and how can it help you become more effective at work?

> Minds are like parachutes. They only function when they are open.
>
> Sir James Dewar

Critical thinking is that which goes beyond the basic recall of information. It is what enables you to utilize your mind's ability to its fullest potential. Every time you weigh one solution against another, analyze possible outcomes to a problem, or brainstorm ideas, you are thinking critically. Although critical thinking is something you probably do everyday, from completing the smallest chore (comparing prices at the grocery store) to handling the most complex situation (managing your budget after a layoff), it is especially important on the job. Your employers will want you to be able to do the following:

- Brainstorm possible solutions to problems.
- Weigh the pros and cons of the different outcomes.
- Analyze which solution should be implemented.
- Assess whether the choice was the right one.

The purpose of this chapter is to help you increase your critical thinking skills. You will also learn the benefits of creative thinking and the importance of developing emotional intelligence. Finally, you will learn the advantages of thinking outside the box—how your vision can inspire your company and those with whom you work to new levels of accomplishment. To view critical thinking in action, consider the story of Izara Moore:

> Izara has just been transferred to Overland Park, Missouri, to take over the department manager position in a major department store chain. The position is a step up for Izara with a large pay increase and additional benefits. Art Holt, the previous manager, will spend two weeks orienting her to the position. Senior management has decided to move Art to a different job because of his ineffective leadership, lack of respect for customers, and his domineering mannerisms. His department has the lowest sales in the country.
>
> Izara is aware that her next two weeks could be difficult. Art has hired everyone on the staff, and Izara guesses that they have a strong allegiance to him. On her first day at the new job, the secretary lets her into Art's office and introduces her arrival. Art is sitting on the corner of his desk. Three other employees are gathered around him. Before Izara can even say "hello," Art quickly dismisses her, saying: "Can't you see I'm in a private meeting here? You'll need to wait outside. In fact, why don't you come back in a few hours? I'll have some time then."

What Izara does next will be a very important step for her. In situations like these, you have to quickly assess the problem, weigh possible outcomes, and forge ahead, adjusting as you go. What would you do?

HOW CAN YOU USE CRITICAL THINKING SKILLS TO SOLVE PROBLEMS?

Every day you are confronted with problems that need solving. Knowing how to approach problems and be able to solve them is a skill you will continue to hone throughout your life. On the job, solving problems is especially important. You will have problems to solve such as how to meet the month end quotas, how to train a new employee, how to tell someone he or she is not performing up to standards, or how to manage a conflict in a staff meeting. How you approach problems will make a difference in how well you do on the job. Your employers will want you to be adept at managing the numerous challenges.

Seven Steps for Effective Decision Making

By following the steps for effective decision making, you will make better decisions. There are seven steps in the process:

State the problem. What exactly is the problem? Be as specific as possible. For instance, you have just been hired at a company several miles away and have determined that you may need transportation. After analyzing your situation, and determining that other modes of transportation are not feasible, you can narrow your statement of the problem down even further. For the purpose of this case, the identified problem is that you need an automobile.

Determine the criteria. What are the important factors to you in the decision you're about to make? In this case, you may determine that the criteria you think are important in looking for a car are the following:

Price
Gas mileage
Style
Comfort

Rate the importance of the criteria. This is not a scientific formula, and you can rate factors in several ways. What you want to do is to quantify your subjective feelings about the factors. One of the easiest ways to rate the importance of each factor is to use a scale of 1 to 10, with 10 being the most important factor to you. For example, in this case, the rating may look something like this:

Price	This is the most important factor, by far, in your decision so you give this a **10**.
Gas mileage	This is important to you, but compared to price, you would rate this as a **5**.
Style	This is very important—and, compared to price and gas mileage, you would rate this as a **7**.
Comfort	This is the least important factor to you, and you give it a rating of **2**.

Brainstorm solutions. Write down as many possible solutions as you can. At this point, don't assess whether the ideas are practical—just let the ideas flow freely without deciding if they're good or bad. For the purpose of illustrating this process, we will use only three possible solutions, though there would, of course, be several more. The possible solutions we will use are the following cars:

Volkswagen Beetle
Jeep Wrangler
Honda Accord

Analyze each possible solution. To analyze the possible solutions, we will rate the possible solutions according to the criteria. For example, we can look at the cars' qualities in terms of price, gas mileage, style, and comfort by developing a chart like chart A below.

Chart A

CRITERIA/ IMPORTANCE	CAR CHOICES		
	Volkswagen Beetle	Jeep Wrangler	Honda Accord
Price			
Gas Mileage			
Style			
Comfort			

Now rate the cars in terms of the criteria. For example, how does a Beetle rank in terms of gas mileage? Again, you can use a scale of 1 to 10, with 10 being the best. After getting information on each car, you might rate the Beetle and the Accord as 8 and 10, respectively, on gas mileage. The Jeep you may rate as 4 because its gas mileage is very low, compared to the other cars. After completing the chart, it may look something like Chart B.

Choose the best solution. At this point, consider whether you have included all of the important criteria. If there are others you would like to include, go back and add them to your chart. Once you have rated all of the possible solutions by criteria, enter the importance of each criteria, which you determined in step 3, on Chart C.

Now multiply the value of the criteria rating by the value you assigned to each possible solution. For example, the Volkswagen Beetle, which you rated

Chart B

CRITERIA/ IMPORTANCE	CAR CHOICES		
	Volkswagen Beetle	Jeep Wrangler	Honda Accord
Price	5	6	7
Gas Mileage	8	4	10
Style	9	10	5
Comfort	6	5	8

Chart C

CRITERIA/ IMPORTANCE	CAR CHOICES		
	Volkswagen Beetle	Jeep Wrangler	Honda Accord
Price	5	6	7
10			
Gas Mileage	8	4	10
5			
Style	9	10	5
7			
Comfort	6	5	8
2			
Total Value			

as 5 for price will be multiplied by the price criteria rating of 10, the total value of which will be 50. Complete the multiplication for each solution and criteria value (see Chart D).

Sum the values for each solution. In this case, the value for the Honda Accord of 171 (70 + 50 + 35 + 16) is higher than any other option. If you selected the criteria and their weights appropriately, then this should be the

Chart D

CRITERIA/ IMPORTANCE	CAR CHOICES		
	Volkswagen Beetle	Jeep Wrangler	Honda Accord
Price	5	6	7
10	50	60	70
Gas Mileage	8	4	10
5	40	20	50
Style	9	10	5
7	63	70	35
Comfort	6	5	8
2	12	10	16
Total Value	165	160	171

solution you choose. By going through this process, even if you choose to implement another solution than the one chosen, you will be more aware of your thinking processes and the value of alternative solutions.

Implement the solution and evaluate the outcome. Once you purchase your car, in this case, or implement any decision, you'll want to evaluate it. There may be other criteria that you might find are important or more important than what you had originally thought. If this is the case, start again at the beginning of the process and state your new problem. For every decision you make, you will want to analyze its outcome. Let's assume that Izara, the new department manager, has an enormous amount of time to deal with her situation. Using the steps described previously, address Izara's situation. Go through the decision-making process for her.

In reality, of course, Izara doesn't have the time to go through this process. She must think quickly and come up with a solution that lays a solid foundation for her position as department manager. Many work decisions will need to be made quickly. The better you are at thinking on your feet or thinking under tense situations, the better you will perform in a position of leadership. If you practice the decision-making process when you have the time, you will think more critically when you are confronted with situations requiring quick action. Also, you can begin to anticipate problems before they occur. Izara, for instance, had thought that she might be walking into a situation where the previous manager had strong employee support. She might have anticipated a need to establish herself as the new leader and gain their respect. With this in mind, what could Izara have done? What would you have done in that position?

Using your mind to come up with effective solutions is a skill. Just like any skill, the more you practice, the better you will become. Brainstorming is one method for increasing your creative problem-solving juices. The following section looks at creative thinking and gives suggestions for increasing your creative abilities.

HOW CAN YOU USE CREATIVE THINKING TO MAKE BETTER DECISIONS?

Creativity is the ability to create something, whether it is a solution, tangible product, work of art, idea, system, program, or format. Everyone is creative in some form or fashion. Some people assume that the word *creative* refers primarily to visual and performing artists–writers, designers, musicians, actors and others who work in creative fields. *Creativity, though, is inside everyone and exists in every field.*

Imagine if part of your day was spent envisioning new products. What would you create? If you're in the aerospace industry, you might think of a way to outfit a plane with a parachute in order to gently drop it to the ground during a mechanical failure. If you're in the automobile industry, you might pursue the idea of solar-powered engines or rubber cars developed for safety. Or you may think of ways to preserve the rain forest for medical research. You can apply creative thinking to any job and come up with innovative ways to increase your company's effectiveness in the marketplace. You can develop your creative thinking skills when you open yourself to a variety of people, seek input from others, and brainstorm.

Open yourself to different types of people. By meeting people from different cultures and people with different skills and likes, you expand your own frame of reference, which gives you a wider array of ideas from which to work.

Solicit input from others. Creative thinking is even more effective when you do it with others. The ideas another person has can spark ideas within your own mind. When your creative juices are tapped, try brainstorming with others.

Brainstorm. Let your mind wander and then write down or talk about the ideas that you have. Detach from the outcome so your mind has the freedom to seek all kinds of solutions. Don't worry if the ideas seem amazing or unreasonable. The point is to first get the ideas flowing.

HOW CAN CREATIVE THINKING HELP SOLVE PROBLEMS?

Whenever issues come up that are difficult to solve, use your creative thinking skills to come up with possible solutions. Give your mind the chance to develop as many ideas as possible without immediately judging them as good or bad. Consider the following rules when seeking solutions.

Don't Evaluate or Criticize an Idea Right Away

Write down your ideas so you remember them. Evaluate them later after you've had a chance to think about them. For instance, your boss has said that you need to develop better relationships with your coworkers. You're a bit of a loner and like your privacy, and you don't really know how to change any more than you already have. You write down several ideas even though they seem unobtainable.

Focus on Quantity and Worry About Quality Later

Try to generate as many solutions as you can. For example, in the hypothetical situation above, you write:

> I could take a seminar in public speaking.
> I could invite people over to my house for a barbecue.
> I could start eating my lunch in the lunchroom instead of my office.
> I could get counseling.
> I could ask my boss how she'd handle the situation if she were me.
> I could change jobs.
> I could tell my boss that even though I'm quiet, I respect people.
> I could begin to learn about people one-on-one.
> I could start asking questions of other people to engage conversation.
> I could watch how others interact and learn from them.

Let Yourself Consider Wild and Unorthodox Ideas

Trust yourself to fall off the edge of tradition when you explore solutions. Sometimes the craziest ideas end up being the most workable solutions.

Assess Your Creativity

Solving problems means you have to think creatively about possible solutions and the effects those solutions will have in your job and in your life. The exercise on the following page can give you a general idea if you're using your creative skills to the greatest advantage.

Now that you have a better understanding of creativity, try using your creative mind when you are attempting to solve problems. Remember, creativity can be developed if you have the desire and patience. The more you practice, the more easily you will be able to come up with creative solutions to the problems you face. These rules are also extremely effective when working with groups. Use creative brainstorming regularly. Your effectiveness at work will increase because of it.

CREATIVITY ASSESSMENT

Circle the number that best describes your situation.

1. How frequently do you explore ideas outside your own interests and expertise?

   Seldom   *Sometimes*   *Often*
   1   2   3   4   5   6   7   8   9   10

2. How frequently do you ask "what if" questions or use impractical ideas as stepping stones to new ideas?

   Seldom   *Sometimes*   *Often*
   1   2   3   4   5   6   7   8   9   10

3. How often do you question assumptions, challenge the rules, or discard obsolete ideas?

   Seldom   *Sometimes*   *Often*
   1   2   3   4   5   6   7   8   9   10

4. How frequently do you use metaphors to generate new ideas?

   Seldom   *Sometimes*   *Often*
   1   2   3   4   5   6   7   8   9   10

5. How frequently are you able to motivate yourself, get rid of excuses, and get your ideas into action?

   Seldom   *Sometimes*   *Often*
   1   2   3   4   5   6   7   8   9   10

Now total your score: _____

If you scored between 45 and 50, you're probably a creative thinker. If you scored lower—don't fret. Remember, creativity can be developed. Creativity expert, Roger von Oech says, "The hallmark of creative people is their mental flexibility." Creative people combine ideas and information in ways that form entirely new solutions, ideas, processes, uses, or products.

In the list below, check those additional characteristics that apply to you.

- _____ Willingness to take risks. For example, taking a difficult high-level course at school or a project at work.
- _____ Tendency to break away from customary limitations. For example, entering a marathon race.
- _____ Tendency to seek challenges and new experiences. For example, taking on an internship in an unfamiliar and high-pressure workplace.
- _____ Broad range of interests in which he or she becomes involved. For example, playing baseball on the company team, volunteering for a food drive, or sitting on an executive board.
- _____ Ability to make unique things out of available materials and objects. For example, writing a poem, motorizing a Lego display, or developing a new packaging product.
- _____ Willingness to deviate from popular opinion. For example, working for a small, relatively unknown political party.
- _____ Curiosity and inquisitiveness. For example, wanting to know how to repair computers, and learning how effective your communication systems are at work.

From *A Whack on the Side of the Head* by Roger van Oech. © Warner Books. Used with permission.

WHAT IS EMOTIONAL INTELLIGENCE AND HOW CAN IT HELP YOU BECOME MORE EFFECTIVE AT WORK?

Many people find problem solving relatively easy when they approach it using critical and creative thinking skills. It can be much more difficult to solve problems, though, when you are emotionally invested in the outcome or are unable to see the situation from an objective perspective.

Would you believe that in an office in California, two people continuously fight over the same thermostat? One person turns it up and the other person turns it back down until they're both so mad you can almost see the steam coming from the tops of their heads. In another office, one employee gossips hatefully about another person, spreading vicious rumors. The person on the receiving end quits the company and later files a lawsuit for a hostile work environment. Cases such as these happen every day in companies across the country. When you bring a group of people together, it is natural to have conflict. How you manage the conflict and how you process your own feelings can make a huge difference in your personal success. Learn to manage your emotional life.

*It is with the heart that one sees clearly,
what is essential is invisible to the mind.*

Antoine de Saint-Exupéry

There are many ways of gathering information. We have multiple intelligences, which affect how we learn, process, store, and retain information. In addition to the research done on these multiple intelligences, Daniel Goleman, author of *Emotional Intelligence*, says that there are two completely different ways of knowing something. Our rational mind is used to comprehend information. We also have an emotional mind, which responds to information through the feelings.

Although it is extremely important to develop your critical and creative thinking skills, having healthy responses to life can be equally important to both your well-being and success. Look at the list of benefits below and imagine how they might help you perform your job more effectively:

- Recognizing other's emotions
- Responding to others with skill
- Knowing how to delay gratification
- Understanding and effectively managing your own responses
- Knowing how to manage your disappointments

When you think about your work at school or in the marketplace, reflect on how you are feeling about what you are doing. Do you feel you have a choice in what you do? Do you feel good about your contributions? Is your work up to your standards or are you feeling inadequate? Have you chosen work that gives you a sense of accomplishment?

IN THE REAL WORLD: John and Carol Newkirk

Everyone expects trials and tribulations in life, but few face adversity with the strength and ingenuity of the Newkirks. In 1967 the Newkirk's daughter, Vickey, developed hydrocephalus, a condition also referred to as water on the brain. After undergoing major brain surgery to implant a shunting device, Vickey was eventually sent home. A few weeks later, though, Vickey insisted on taking a bike ride. She crashed, hitting her head against the ground. She was rushed back to the local emergency room where doctors informed John and Carol Newkirk that a second surgery might have to be performed to clear the now clogged and bleeding shunting device that had been inserted into their three-year-old's head just weeks before. In addition, they would likely have to schedule yet another surgery to do the same thing the following year.

Both the Newkirks and the doctors were upset that there wasn't a shunt that could be manually cleared of blood and clogging without performing the delicate surgery all over again. Vickey's father, a chemistry professor and specialist in physical metallurgy, immediately began the race against time to develop this type of shunt, which could be used on Vickey in time for her surgery the following year.

Within a year Dr. Newkirk had developed a shunt that would work. After consulting with the neurosurgeons working with Vickey, the device was improved and eventually patented. Carol Newkirk began manufacturing what came to be known as the Denver Hydrocephalus Shunt working in the kitchen of their home. Vickey's condition healed naturally, and she never needed the additional surgery or the shunt her father had worked so desperately to invent. They donated the first two hundred shunts, until surgeons began calling and requesting the shunt by name. That was when they began their first company, Denver Biomaterials, Inc.

Amid all of the worry about Vickey and the excitement and triumph surrounding the invention, the Newkirk's oldest son disappeared. After on-going efforts to locate him, his body was discovered in California almost a year later. Carol said, "We were at the absolute bottom of discouragement." But Dr. Newkirk summed it up by saying

> The definition of success is getting up one more time than you've been knocked down. How many times have people fallen down or failed and yet still found a way to rise with courage? It's what we're all capable of.

Dr. Newkirk was then asked if he could create a shunt small enough to be inserted into the brain of an unborn fetus who was developing water on the brain. In April of 1981, after just three days, he developed the first fetal shunt, and successful surgery was performed soon thereafter at Colorado's University Hospital, making headline news all over the world.

Six other shunts were all developed not long afterwards. The business grew and was eventually sold to Johnson and Johnson in 1986. However, the sale of his company was not the end of Dr. Newkirk's inventions and contributions to the medical community. He now heads up Colorado Biomedical, Inc. where he markets a microdissection needle, his latest invention.

When asked if he ever felt like just giving up when facing tragedy, Dr. Newkirk remarked,

> What are the alternatives when you face adversity? If you quit, where does that lead you? You are going to have problems. Just identify them, seek a reasonable solution that you are capable of meeting, and work at it—don't ever give up!

Empowerment Inventory

The following assessment developed by Kenneth Thomas and Walter Tymon Jr. can help you discover whether you are feeling good about the work you are currently performing. You can use it to address a specific project or give you overall feedback to your general degree of satisfaction. By using the inventory, you are learning to develop your emotional intelligence.

Below are 24 statements describing a variety of feelings you might have about your tasks. For each statement, please circle the number, from 1 to 7, that best describes how strongly you agree or disagree with that statement.

Please do not skip any of the items. Although some of the statements appear to be similar, your answer to each of them is important.

EMPOWERMENT INVENTORY

	Strongly Agree				Strongly Disagree		
1. I am making good progress on my projects.	1	2	3	4	5	6	7
2. I am good at my job.	1	2	3	4	5	6	7
3. I care about what I'm doing.	1	2	3	4	5	6	7
4. I feel free to select different paths or approaches in my work.	1	2	3	4	5	6	7
5. I am proficient at what I am doing.	1	2	3	4	5	6	7
6. I have a sense that things are moving along well.	1	2	3	4	5	6	7
7. My work serves a valuable purpose.	1	2	3	4	5	6	7
8. How I go about doing things is up to me.	1	2	3	4	5	6	7
9. My projects are going well.	1	2	3	4	5	6	7
10. My projects are significant to me.	1	2	3	4	5	6	7
11. I am performing competently.	1	2	3	4	5	6	7
12. I have a sense of freedom in what I am doing.	1	2	3	4	5	6	7
13. The work I am doing is important.	1	2	3	4	5	6	7
14. I am doing my work capably.	1	2	3	4	5	6	7
15. I am accomplishing my objectives.	1	2	3	4	5	6	7
16. I am determining what I do on my job.	1	2	3	4	5	6	7
17. I am skillful in my work.	1	2	3	4	5	6	7
18. What I am trying to accomplish is meaningful to me.	1	2	3	4	5	6	7
19. I feel I have a lot of latitude in what I am doing.	1	2	3	4	5	6	7
20. My tasks are moving forward.	1	2	3	4	5	6	7
21. I am doing worthwhile things.	1	2	3	4	5	6	7
22. I am exercising a lot of choice in what I do.	1	2	3	4	5	6	7
23. I am doing things well.	1	2	3	4	5	6	7
24. My work is proceeding nicely.	1	2	3	4	5	6	7

Adapted from the Empowerment Inventory Instrument, © 1993, by Xicom, Inc., Tuxedo, NY. Reproduced with permission by Prentice-Hall, Inc.

CHAPTER 4   CRITICAL AND CREATIVE THINKING   **69**

Scoring the empowerment inventory. Fill in the appropriate number for each of the questionnaire's 24 items. For instance, if you answered **3** for question 1, place a 3 in the box provided by number 1 below. When you are finished, add up the scores in each column.

	Feelings of Choice	Feelings of Competence	Feelings of Meaningfulness	Feelings of Progress
1.				☐
2.		☐		
3.			☐	
4.	☐			
5.		☐		
6.				☐
7.			☐	
8.	☐			
9.				☐
10.			☐	
11.		☐		
12.	☐			
13.			☐	
14.		☐		
15.				☐
16.	☐			
17.		☐		
18.			☐	
19.	☐			
20.				☐
21.			☐	
22.	☐			
23.		☐		
24.				☐

Total the scores in each column.

Choice	Competence	Meaningfulness	Progress
☐	☐	☐	☐

If you scored 36 or above for choice, you are in the top-25 percentile.
If you scored 39 or above for competence, you are in the top-25 percentile.
If you scored 37 or above for meaningfulness, you are in the top-25 percentile.
If you scored 36 or above for progress, you are in the top-25 percentile.

If you scored 25 to 35 for choice, you are in the middle-50 percentile.
If you scored 34 to 38 for competence, you are in the middle-50 percentile.
If you scored 29 to 36 for meaningfulness, you are in the middle-50 percentile.
If you scored 29 to 35 for progress, you are in the middle-50 percentile.

If you scored 0 to 24 for choice, you are in the low-25 percentile.
If you scored 0 to 33 for competence, you are in the low-25 percentile.
If you scored 0 to 28 for meaningfulness, you are in the low-25 percentile.
If you scored 0 to 28 for progress, you are in the low-25 percentile.

So what does all of this mean?

> **Choice** is the opportunity you feel to select task activities that make sense to you and to perform them in ways that seem appropriate. The feeling of choice is the feeling of being free to choose—of being able to use your own judgment and act out of your own understanding of the task.
>
> **Competence** is the accomplishment you feel in skillfully performing task activities you have chosen. The feeling of competence involves the sense that you are doing good, quality work on a task.
>
> **Meaningfulness** is the opportunity you feel to pursue a worthy task purpose. The feeling of meaningfulness is the feeling that you are on a path that is worth your time and energy—that you are on a valuable mission, that your purpose matters in the larger scheme of things.
>
> **Progress** is the accomplishment you feel in achieving the task purpose. The feeling of progress involves the sense that the task is moving forward, that your activities are really accomplishing something.

Applying the Four Feelings of Empowerment

When you understand your feelings about the job you are doing, you are more able to alter your path than if the job is progressing poorly or you feel frustrated by your contributions. In addition, if you assess how others around you feel about their contributions or the project in general, you have a better chance of affecting positive changes in the work environment.

Imagine how frustrating a project would be if no one was willing to discuss how they felt, acting as if everything was progressing normally when it was not. Some companies and individual departments operate just that way. As an employee of such a company, you'll eventually feel frustrated by the unspoken reality. To avoid this, learn to say what you feel. Ask others for feedback. Create an environment where expressing feelings about work—positive or not—is expected and acceptable.

Self-Mastery

Listed below are additional qualities found in those people who have successfully developed their emotional life. Check the ones you feel are strengths of yours. Leave the others blank if you feel you need to give that area extra attention.

People who have gained mastery over their emotional life

_____ are aware of their moods

_____ have control over their emotional life

_____ are generally self-sufficient

_____ are in good psychological health

_____ recognize and respect their personal needs

_____ manage bad days with relative ease

_____ do not obsess

_____ know how to ask for help

_____ forgive quickly

_____ look for the good in every situation

_____ feel a sense of joy about their lives

If these qualities are yours, congratulations. You are probably feeling good about your participation in life and with others. If not, don't worry. At some point, most people have to deal with situations that challenge their sense of well-being or confidence. When those times arise, recognize that you have power over the situation; you can make choices that will relieve or even alleviate the problem altogether. Use your critical thinking and creative thinking to discover your alternatives—then move ahead knowing what you can do to change your life for the better.

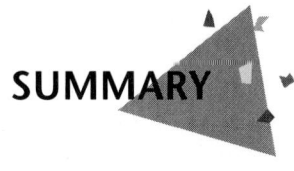

SUMMARY

Successful people utilize their minds as powerful resources.

Awareness is the first, and perhaps, greatest quality one can have when attempting to solve problems on the job or in life in general. By opening your mind, you can see the situation from many perspectives—perspectives that may be different or even better than your own. You then can more easily understand how you and others might be affected by the situation. You can imagine different outcomes or make adjustments while a project is in progress.

The seven steps for effective problem solving are listed below:

State the problem.
Determine the criteria.
Rate the criteria.
Brainstorm solutions.
Analyze each solution.
Choose the best solution.
Implement the solution and evaluate the outcome.

If you want to effectively overcome obstacles, spend some time getting to know yourself emotionally. Learn to use your mind to critically assess problems and potential outcomes. And finally, develop your creative side. Let your mind take you to new levels of success.

Applications & Exercises

PERSONAL ASSETS

YOUR EMOTIONAL HEALTH

Following is an emotional intelligence inventory. Read through the lists and circle the appropriate response for each item. When you are finished, look over the different responses and note the areas where you are strong and the areas where you need improvement.

SELF AWARENESS

I notice what I'm feeling throughout the day.	Never	Usually	Always
I am able to take appropriate action based on the feelings I'm having.	Never	Usually	Always
When I am confused about my feelings, I seek assistance from a friend, family member, or professional.	Never	Usually	Always
When I am angry or hurt, I am able to control myself and not lash out at others.	Never	Usually	Always
I am comfortable sharing what I'm feeling with others.	Never	Usually	Always
I have dealt effectively with the significant losses and traumas of my life.	Never	Usually	Always

OTHER AWARENESS

When someone else is upset, I am able to listen without feeling threatened.	Never	Usually	Always
I can recognize anger just by looking at a person's body language.	Never	Usually	Always
I am able to give constructive criticism effectively.	Never	Usually	Always
When someone is crying, I can offer comfort without feeling uneasy.	Never	Usually	Always
I am comfortable in group settings.	Never	Usually	Always
I am patient with others.	Never	Usually	Always
My friends discuss their emotions with me.	Never	Usually	Always

If you answered "never" to any of the categories, it is a clear indication that you need to spend some quality time and effort developing those skills. There are many wonderful tools you can use to help you increase your emotional

health—read self-help books, talk to close friends or family members, or get professional help from a coach or a counselor.

If you answered "usually" to any of the statements, you are probably doing just fine. Practice staying aware of your actions and behaviors. That way, you'll be able to increase your effectiveness on those occasions when you feel challenged by your work or those with whom you interact.

If you answered "always" you probably have a positive and effective outlook on life. Keep up the good work, continue to pay attention to your emotional life, and give back to others so they can learn to do the same.

WORKING TOGETHER

Brainstorming in Action

Move into small groups and practice your brainstorming and creative thinking skills. Your assignment is to find a solution to the following problem:

> Your company manufactures shoes. It is a family-run business and has developed a positive image in the shoe business over the years. Now, however, the competitors are doing so well that you have lost your market share. How can you update your product and regain your footing in the shoe market?

Begin by jotting down ten ideas that come to mind regarding the topic. Don't analyze whether they are good responses or not. When you are finished share your responses with your group. Then have the group continue the process aloud until you come up with the responses you like the best.

CASE STUDIES

What Would You Do?

Your company produces educational software. Sales have been slow for the past year. For some reason the schools are not latching onto the products. You know that if they do, your market share will increase dramatically. What can you do? In the space provided, quickly jot down at least five ideas no matter how fantastic or seemingly unrealistic.

When you are finished writing down your ideas, move into groups of three to five people and share your ideas. As a group, decide on the top three choices. Now return to the large group and share your top three with the others. When every group is finished sharing, identify the three best solutions for the entire class. Write them on the board. Now, tally which solution is the one that the group thinks is best.

Two

Fontana has just been transferred to your division. You'll be working closely with him on several projects in the next few months. Although he seems like a nice enough guy, you're not sure if he's going to fit in with the rest of the team. He seems pretty controlled and somewhat rigid in his thinking. You're afraid he's too logical and linear in his approach. At the first team meeting you noticed that he became very uncomfortable when you opened the floor for discussion. You've also noticed that he seems frustrated with how the rest of the group does business. You know he comes highly recommended as an individual who can get the work accomplished. How can you help him fit into the team? What should you address? Pair off with another student and write your suggestions in the space provided. When you are finished, return to the rest of the class for a general discussion.

Expressing Yourself and Understanding Others

Learning to Communicate Effectively

KEY CONCEPTS

- What are the basics of effective communication?
- How can you develop good communication skills?
- What are some of the barriers to communication?
- How can you use good communication skills in conflict resolution?

> We have two ears and only one tongue that we may hear more and speak less.
>
> Diogenes

Communication is a significant part of our everyday lives and is really the lifeline of any organization. Dr. Charles Beck, a managerial communications professor at the University of Colorado at Denver defines communication as "a transactional process in which people exchange ideas, information, feeling, attitudes, or impressions." He likens communication to a lifeline, connecting people within an organization while providing a means of connecting to others outside the organization.

People cannot *not* communicate—even silence conveys attitudes and values as interpreted by others. However, if a supportive communication climate is fostered, and people have good communication skills, organizational effectiveness will increase. The purpose of this chapter is to bring your personal communication abilities to the forefront, giving you the opportunity to examine these communication practices and either change them for the better or enhance what already works.

Communication is as complex and varied as the types of people who communicate. Although verbal communication is the most widely used, we also communicate with nonverbal signals such as body language or sighs. In addition, just as your learning style affects how you take in and process information, a learning style also affects the way in which you communicate. If you've ever seen people who can't seem to talk without using their hands, you've probably witnessed a kinesthetic learner in action. In the same vein, an auditory learner may be very sensitive to your tone of voice or may communicate using references to how things sound to them. If you're a visual learner, you may notice people's nonverbal signals or may use visual images as you "paint" your way through a conversation. Just as you are a unique individual with a distinct way of communicating with others, everyone you meet also has his or her own unique communication style.

Consider the story of Jameson Williams.

> Jameson grew up in an inner-city community. For him, life consisted of going to school (just a few blocks from home), playing basketball after school and on weekends, studying, and going to the First Baptist Church on Sundays with his grandmother. When his family got a call from the school indicating Jameson had won a scholarship to a prestigious university due to his extremely high academic scores, his family was quite proud. Although Jameson was hesitant to leave, he really wanted the chance to excel. He accepted the scholarship and moved to his new school. "The first year was hell for me," he reflected years later. "I just didn't fit in. It wasn't so much being a minority that was the problem. I just couldn't talk to people like I used to. Hardly anyone understood the words or experiences that were so familiar to me."

In local groups such as families, towns, communities, and regions of the country, languages can develop that are unique to the area. Moving away from these communities can be challenging. Acclimating to a new culture and a new way of communicating (even though you may speak the same basic language) can be difficult and time-consuming. This phenomenon doesn't just happen within cultural centers. Many businesses have language that is industry-specific. For example, perhaps you've listened to a group of computer programmers discuss the latest in computer technology or listened to musicians talk about the chord progressions they're going to use in a song—the jargon used may enhance communication within a group while hindering communication among groups.

When you consider the differing cultural backgrounds of people and the different experiences that influence their lives, you begin to understand why effective communication can be difficult to achieve. How then can diverse people, molded from numerous experiences and social influences, relate to one another without confusion?

WHAT ARE THE BASICS OF EFFECTIVE COMMUNICATION?

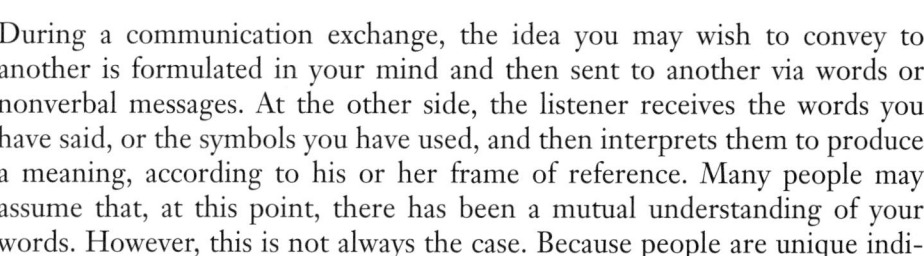

During a communication exchange, the idea you may wish to convey to another is formulated in your mind and then sent to another via words or nonverbal messages. At the other side, the listener receives the words you have said, or the symbols you have used, and then interprets them to produce a meaning, according to his or her frame of reference. Many people may assume that, at this point, there has been a mutual understanding of your words. However, this is not always the case. Because people are unique individuals with unique historical frameworks, words can be misinterpreted and meanings can be misconstrued.

One of your jobs as an effective communicator, then, is to practice formulating your ideas as clearly as possible before you send them—think before you speak. If you know anything about the person who is on the receiving end of your communication (whether that person is overly sensitive, dislikes "you" messages, is mistrustful of your leadership, etc.), remember to phrase your ideas carefully keeping those things in mind. If you are in a leadership position, it is especially important to think before you speak. Your communication, coupled with your position of power, can make it more difficult for people to really hear what you are saying. The following strategies can help you verbalize your message successfully:

Think Before You Speak

What are the implications of saying what is on your mind? Spoken too soon, your ideas can come out sounding nothing like you intended. Spoken without considering how your communication may affect others may cause unnecessary conflict or confusion. A little extra thought (and even some private rehearsal) can help you choose the perfect moment and combination of words.

Be Clear, Precise, and Honest

Decide the main point of what you want to say and state it clearly. Link your ideas to examples, avoiding any extra information that can distract from the heart of the message. No one can really respond to your ideas until you present them clearly and honestly.

Communicate within a Reasonable Time Frame

One danger of holding back is that the problem you are addressing may increase in severity if you wait. Another is that when you don't express yourself, anger may increase and emerge when you least expect it. Wait until you have gathered and organized your thoughts, then look for the opportunity to communicate.

Communicate with Respect

No matter how old or young, people deserve to be treated with respect. Even if you're extremely upset or feel justified, monitor your words. Although it may be tempting to dive into a conflict, by resisting the temptation to use harsh words, you will feel better about yourself and make it easier to salvage a damaged relationship.

HOW CAN YOU DEVELOP GOOD COMMUNICATION SKILLS?

Develop Listening Skills

The act of hearing isn't the same as the act of listening. While hearing refers to sensing sounds and words, listening involves a complex process of communication. Successful listening results in the speaker's intended ideas reaching the listener. On the job, poor listening can result in communication breakdowns that cause project delays, missed appointments, customer dissatisfaction, and poor team relations. Good listening, on the other hand, can be the greatest contributor to your success on the job. The chart below shows the stages of listening.

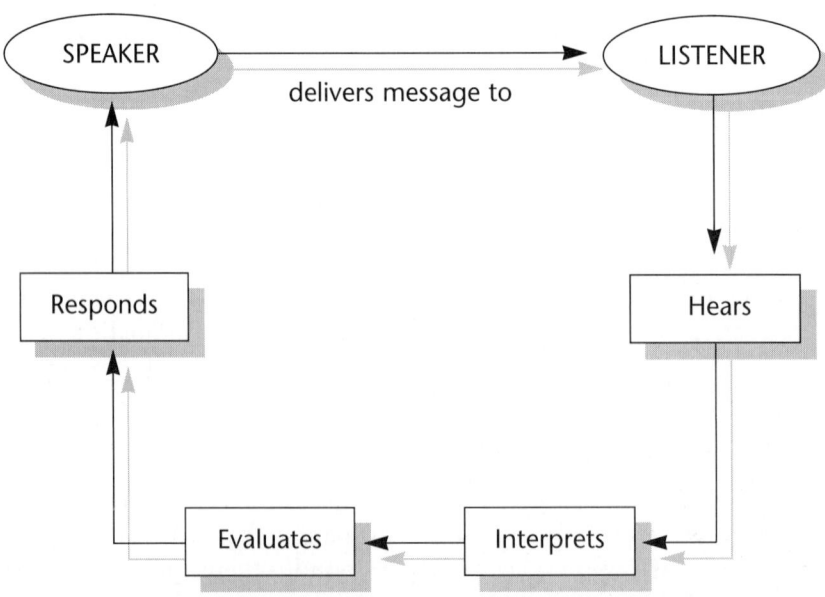

Listening is accomplished through a series made up of four stages: hearing, interpreting, evaluating, and responding. These stages take the information from the sender (speaker) to the receiver (listener) and back again.

> In the first stage, a listener **HEARS**—sound waves enter the ears and are transmitted as signals to the brain. For example, you are sitting in a meeting and hear your boss say: "The next market research report will be due on Friday at one o'clock. There will be no exceptions."
>
> In the second stage **INTERPRETATION** occurs. Listeners gather meaning from the message. For example, when you heard the due date of the report, you might have remembered how much work went into the report you did last month and expect that a similar report is required.
>
> In the **EVALUATION** stage of listening, feelings are assigned to the message—whether, for example, you agree with it or find it objectionable. This involves relating the message to your needs and values. In this example, you may think that, with the due date for other current projects, you don't have enough time to complete this report by Friday, and you may begin to feel a little stressed.
>
> The final stage of listening involves **RESPONDING** in the form of direct feedback. Your reaction, in this example, may be to ask questions. By doing this, you might be able to determine that your boss does not want the same type of report as last month, and is only interested in the new sales figures, which is a less time-consuming project.

While all of these stages are essential for effective communication, perhaps the most important is the final stage—responding. It is from your response that the speaker will be able to judge if you have effectively understood. Whenever you communicate, make sure you ask for feedback from the listener(s). If you have been misunderstood, you'll still have time to correct the problem. If you don't ask, you won't really know what people thought about what you said.

Overcome Listening Challenges

Studies have shown that when a manager speaks to an employee, only 33 percent of the content is retained, and the rest is forgotten. There are many reasons for this. People have divided attention, listening challenges, and/or disabilities that limit effective listening. Still, people can learn to manage the challenges of effective listening.

Guy Lounsbury, chief of prosthetics at a government hospital, is paid well for his expertise. Unfortunately, the hospital is crowded with every space used and there is no hope of immediate expansion. Guy's office is tucked in a corner of the hospital. There are four desks for him and his staff, one window and one door. Because the space is so small, the door remains open during office hours. Noise from the hallway filters in throughout the workday. Four phones in one office, people poking their heads in the door to ask for directions, and one-on-one meetings make the office situation close to impossible—and still, they manage. Why?

Guy says it's because he and his staff have learned to tune out conversations other people are having in the room. They work well together because they are able to respect the need for quiet when required and ignore the noise when it intrudes. Without selective hearing, they wouldn't survive in the close quarters. Fortunately for them, they rose to the challenge.

To help create a positive listening environment, explore how you can manage these listening challenges.

Accept responsibility for listening. Your ability to listen well begins with your willingness and commitment to become a good listener. By accepting responsibility, you recognize that understanding others falls on your shoulders. You are the one who needs to listen for the speaker's meaning and question what you don't understand.

Deal with distractions. In business meetings, there can be much to distract you from what the speaker is saying. You may have internal distractions (hunger) or external distractions (noise from a light fixture or someone's stomach growling). If you want to be a good listener, able to understand and retain what is being said, manage the distractions around you. Like the people in Guy Lounsbury's office, learn to have selective hearing—hearing what is important and disregarding superficial noises.

Stay open-minded. Nothing so effectively shuts down our minds as when we disagree with someone. When you are listening and hear something that goes against your values or opinion, work at keeping your mind open to what else the speaker has to say. If it really bothers you, write down a question you can ask on a note pad and then get back to listening. Otherwise, you'll miss what the speaker is saying while you're fuming over what was previously said.

Imagine a construction site surrounded by a fence. Inside the fence is the truth of the matter. When you look through a knothole in the fence, you see the truth from your perspective. Your neighbor looks into a different knot hole, sees the same truth, but from an entirely different perspective. Who knows the real truth? Both of you. If you can remember that everyone's opinion matters, you'll be on your way to healthy communication.

Manage any listening disabilities. Good listening techniques don't always solve every listening problem. People who have a partial hearing loss have a physical explanation for why listening is difficult. If you have hearing loss, seek help from a medical professional. Other disabilities, such as attention deficit disorder (ADD) or a problem processing language, can inhibit you from hearing all that is being said. People with such disabilities have to work exceptionally hard at hearing. As a speaker, you can help people with disabilities by speaking clearly and slowly and having your thoughts well-organized.

Develop Nonverbal Communication Skills

Your actions are a basic form of communication. Even people who cannot speak each other's language can communicate through gestures and facial expressions. Your gestures, eye movement, facial expression, body positioning and posture, touching behavior, and use of personal space are all types of nonverbal communication, also called body language. If you understand how it works, you can use nonverbal communication to your advantage.

Proxemics (distance between communicators). Where you stand when you speak to another person or group says a lot about your comfort level. In the United States, there is an unspoken distance that is used for different circumstances. In some countries, the distances will be different—usually closer. In the United States, generally acceptable distances are the following:

Touching to 18 inches	Family members, lovers, close friends
3 feet	Normal conversational distance
3 feet to 12 feet	Formal or business meetings
12 feet and more	Public presentations

If you find someone standing too close to you, it can be disconcerting. Quietly back up until you have the distance that makes you comfortable. Some people use proxemics as a way to intimidate others. If someone is angry with you and they begin to close the space between you, you probably have an aggressive situation on your hands. At that point, you should speak up and let them know you need more space in order to think through what is being said.

Physical behaviors. The way people use their bodies to communicate is fascinating. By watching people you can discover how well the information has been received, whether they are angry, frustrated, or bored, whether they are distracted, feeling powerful or inadequate, and so on. Imagine walking into the office of your new boss. He doesn't get up when you enter and invite you to sit. Instead, he is leaning back in his chair, arms folded atop his head, with one foot on his desk. What does this say to you? Figure 5.1 provides some possible nonverbal clues.

In addition to your physical behaviors, what you wear can also be a nonverbal clue for those around you. Teenagers are notorious for dressing in outlandish clothing to break from the traditional roles established by their parents and society in general. Most of us expect that kind of behavior from teenagers. But what about at work? If you arrive in a T-shirt and jeans and everyone else is in business attire, what are you saying? In the same vein, if your company promotes casual dress for the employees but the managers all dress in business suits, what are they telling you?

Seating arrangements. Besides clothing, where you sit is also a statement. When you enter a meeting room, notice where you sit in relation to others. If there's just two of you, more than likely you'll sit across from one another or at right angles to each other. If you're in a large group it's better to sit in a circle. Large groups interact better in a circular pattern. If you are in competition with someone or at odds with a coworker, you will generally choose to sit as far away from them as you can but still within their line of vision. Watch where people sit, the distance they put between themselves and others in the room, and how they maintain their field of vision. If they sit close, keep their eyes engaged, and show interest in one another, they probably are engaged in the conversation.

Figure 5.1 *Nonverbal clues.*

Person is glaring.	He or she is probably angry.
Person looks away when you speak.	He or she is probably distracted or uninterested in what you are saying.
Person does not acknowledge you when you walk by.	He or she is either very distracted or upset or is unfriendly.
Person rolls his or her eyes when you speak.	He or she thinks what you're saying is ludicrous.
Person yawns when you talk to him or her.	Either the person did not get enough sleep or the person is bored with what you have to say.
Person leans back and folds his or arms across the chest.	The person has probably made up his or her mind regarding what you are asking or saying.
Person is walking quickly with head down.	Don't disturb this person; he or she wants to be left alone.
Person sighs.	What you are saying is overwhelming the person or the person disagrees with what is being said.
Person leans over you when you are at your desk.	If the person is a manager, the leaning can be an intimidation to see if you've gotten the work done, or a genuine interest in your work. If it is a close friend or coworker, the leaning could mean he or she is interested in what you are doing.
Person continues to read or fails to acknowledge you when you enter the room.	The person is saying that what they are doing is more important than greeting you.

Communication Skills for Business and Professions by Timm and Stead, © 1996. Reprinted by permission of Prentice-Hall, Inc., Upper Saddle River, NJ.

Office arrangements. How supervisors arrange their offices will say a lot about how they view their position. If there are numerous plaques on the wall, your supervisor is probably proud of the accomplishments he or she has achieved. If the desk acts as a barrier between the supervisor and employees, the supervisor might be trying to reinforce his or her position of authority. If you are trying to create an inviting office space that puts people at ease, try the following:

- Come out from behind your desk when people enter. It shows them that you are glad they're there.
- Create an area in your office where you and members of your staff can interact comfortably (perhaps two or three chairs seated next to each other with a coffee table or lamp table nearby).
- Turn your desk at an angle instead of directly in front of the door. People are more likely to feel welcome.

IN THE REAL WORLD: STUART SCOTT

With his pearly grin and charismatic personality, 32-year-old Stuart Scott co-hosts ESPN's *SportsCenter.* Termed "El Fuego" (the fire) by a recent article in Esquire magazine, Stuart has helped make the somewhat comical sports show just about the hottest thing going. How did this young African American get so big, so fast? Well, according to Stuart, it was a gamble.

> I followed the same path of hard work and serious pursuit that everyone who wants to be a TV sports anchor does. I graduated from the University of North Carolina with a degree in speech communications and radio, television, and motion pictures. I worked at the student radio station, WXYC-FM, as a sports and news reporter. And I played football.

Stuart worked as a sports reporter for WESH-TV in Orlando where in just three short years he had won first place honors from the Central Florida Press Club for one of his feature stories. He got his big break with ESPN, the world leader in sports coverage, when he was signed on as anchor of the growing ESPN2 network.

It didn't take long for Stuart to become El Fuego and move on to *SportsCenter.* He admits that he faced some serious controversy over his approach and distinctive street-style delivery of sports. In a recent interview with *Esquire* magazine, Stuart commented to his critics, "I have to walk a tighter line. I do recognize that there is an African American audience that relates to me simply because I'm black and because my style is familiar to them. I'm doing it purposefully to prove that you can be diverse and do this job.

Scott's mother was a school teacher and his father worked for the postal service in Chicago. Scott knows that they were an important part of his success. They demanded hard work from him and also encouraged him to do anything he wanted to do. It is clear that Stuart's parents instilled the kind of confidence in him that has led to his success at *SportsCenter.*

> I know there are and were people out there who thought, "this guy will never make it," but I knew I could. I also knew I was going to have to work extra hard to do the sportscasts my way. But that's my style and that's part of who I am.

Stuart says you still have to do the hard work to become successful. And he recognizes that he has had just as many bad nights on the show as anyone else. "You have bad nights and you go on," he says. It is apparent that Stuart really has gone on. His popularity only continues to grow and his opportunities seem limitless.

WHAT ARE SOME OF THE BARRIERS TO COMMUNICATION?

More and more, diversity is part of your community, your school, your workplace, your family, and what you see on television and access on the Internet. It used to be that most people lived in societies with others who seemed very similar to them. Now, differences among people are woven into everyday life. You may encounter examples of diversity like these:

- Communities with people from differing stages of life
- Coworkers who represent a variety of ethnic origins

- Classmates who speak a number of different languages
- Social situations featuring people from various cultures, religions, and sexual orientations
- Individuals who marry a person or adopt a child from a different racial or religious background
- Diverse restaurants, services, and businesses in the community
- Neighborhoods with immigrants from a variety of social-class backgrounds
- A variety of lifestyles reflected in books, magazines, newspapers, music, and movies, on television, on the Internet, and in other forms of popular culture
- People in the workplace who may have a disability of some type

Remember the following points as you think about your own feelings of living in a diverse world:

1. The world has always been a diverse place. With the onset of global communication and world travel, people are now exposed to all these different types of people and lifestyles.
2. Our effectiveness in the marketplace depends on our ability to interact with diverse populations.
3. Businesses are looking for people who have experience with other cultures to expand their share of the global market.

When people see others as less, lump people into categories, or prevent them from having opportunities, they are denying people their basic right to be respected and valued as human beings. For instance, if a 32-year-old woman is denied a job because the interviewer thinks she'll soon become pregnant, or a 55-year-old man can't get hired because he is considered too old, or a senior female manager gets passed by every time a promotion is available because it is believed that only men should be top executives, the espousers of these opinions are acting in a prejudiced and discriminatory way. By acting in this way, we deny a company all of the benefits that can come from diversity. Stereotypes, prejudice, and discrimination all can form barriers to communication.

Stereotypes

A stereotype occurs when an assumption is made about a person or group of people, based on one or more characteristics. Somebody may think that men with long hair are irresponsible because they met one man with long hair who acted in such a manner. To take characteristics of one member of a group and apply those characteristics to all members of that group is to stereotype. Try to fight this tendency and see each person as a unique individual.

Prejudice

Prejudice occurs when people "prejudge" something, meaning that they make a judgment before they have sufficient knowledge upon which to base that judgment. People often form prejudiced opinions on the basis of a particular characteristic—gender, race, culture, abilities, sexual orientation, religion, and so on. Any group can be subject to prejudice, although certain groups have more often been on the receiving end of such close-minded attitudes.

Discrimination

Discrimination occurs when people deny others opportunities because of their perceived differences and is often accompanied by prejudice. Discrimination can result in the denial of jobs or advancement, equal education opportunities, equal housing opportunities, services, event access, rights, privileges, and commodities.

What Can You Do?

Successful interaction with the people around you can make a positive and lasting difference in the quality of your life. Success, though, depends upon your willingness to be open-minded and to accept differences. In your job you will certainly have to learn to adapt to all kinds of people. If your company operates on the international level, you'll definitely benefit yourself and your employers if you take some time learning about people from other cultures. More importantly, you should learn about the people with whom you work on a daily basis.

More than likely, you will be working alongside people who have different religious affiliations, different lifestyles, different ethnic backgrounds, different abilities, and different value systems. One of your responsibilities as an employee will be to learn how to work effectively with everyone your company hires. Not always an easy task—but one that can be accomplished by following a few basic rules.

- **Avoid judging people on external characteristics and things they can't change.** These include skin color, weight, facial features, or gender.
- **Cultivate relationships with people of different cultures, races, perspectives, and ages.** Find out how other people live and think, and see what you can learn from them.
- **Educate yourself and others.** Take advantage of books and people to teach you about cultures. Empowerment comes through education. If you remain ignorant and blind to the critical issues of race and humanity, you will have no power to influence positive change. Read about other people and cultures.
- **Be sensitive to the needs of others.** Think critically about their situations. Try to put yourself in their place asking yourself questions about what you would feel and do if you were in a similar situation.

- **Look for common ground.** Find similarities in your lives and experiences—parenting, classes, personal challenges, and interests.
- **Practice listening to other people who have different perspectives from your own.** Acknowledge that everyone has a right to their opinion.
- **Take responsibility for making changes instead of pointing the finger at someone else.** Avoid blaming the problems in your life on certain groups or people.
- **Recognize that people everywhere have the same basic needs.** Everyone loves, thinks, hurts, hopes, fears, and plans. People are united through their essential humanity.

HOW CAN YOU USE GOOD COMMUNICATION SKILLS IN CONFLICT RESOLUTION?

The primary key to conflict resolution is calm and open communication.

Effective speaking skills, active listening, and a good understanding of nonverbal communication can help in resolving conflicts. In addition, there are also other techniques available to help in resolving situations where conflict exists. Think about a time when you experienced conflict. You probably were frustrated that the other person wouldn't agree with your point of view. Rarely do people agree on everything all the time. When disagreements cause a communication breakdown, the sooner you deal with it, the better. Eventually, everyone must deal with conflict. Use this section as an opportunity to hone your conflict management and negotiation skills. It will pay off in future interactions.

Conflict is one of the toughest hurdles you will encounter in your relationships. Whether large or small, conflicts arise from a clash of ideas or interests. You may have a small conflict with a roommate over leaving the kitchen messy or leaving doors unlocked. On the other hand, you may have a serious argument over a financial arrangement you made with another person. Conflict can stimulate anger and frustration that shut down lines of communication and create hostile barriers that may stay up for a long time.

Some people handle conflict by lashing out with a vengeance. Others quietly stew. Others repress their feelings and hope the conflict resolves itself on its own. Still others strive to protect their egos at all costs, making it almost impossible for others to be heard. Each of these methods has inherent problems:

> If you *lash out*, you can say something you'll really regret. Hold your tongue until you have carefully thought through what you want to say and why.
>
> If you *give people the silent treatment* while making sure they know how upset you are, it will only exacerbate the problem. Learn to talk calmly about what you're feeling.
>
> If you *repress your feelings*, you are more prone to suffer long-term physical challenges such as stress and certain diseases. Learn to talk about what you feel instead of turning inwards on yourself.

If you are *busy protecting your own ego,* you'll miss what others are saying. Learn to listen and really hear another person's perspective. Take down the barriers around you and let people in.

Conflict can also be a very positive event if handled well. It can shed new light on ideas and strengthen bonds between those involved. Learn to develop your emotional intelligence skills and use them whenever conflict arises.

The primary key to conflict resolution is calm and open communication. If you can diffuse the situation by agreeing to get back to one another after you've thought things through, or agree to listen and respect the other's viewpoint as you talk your way through the conflict, you will have a good shot at negotiation. Certainly, this is not always an easy accomplishment. If it were, the court system wouldn't need to hire trained conflict resolutionists and opposing countries wouldn't go to war. Hopefully, though, by using the following suggestions, your conflicts can be resolved with relative ease.

Set the ground rules before a problem occurs. Even before you begin working together, discuss how you will handle problems when they arise. Make agreements and then keep them during conflict. If a conflict comes up and you haven't discussed the ground rules, stop the conflict and take a moment to decide how you will progress. Although this may sound impractical, especially when you're in the heat of the moment, taking a few minutes to set the rules is the most important thing you can do in an argument.

Resolve the conflict when the involved parties are calm. Occasionally, it is better to walk away and approach the problem at a different time. Agree on a set time to discuss the issues again before you part. Spend your time thinking about what you want to say and how that may be interpreted.

Take turns stating what you are feeling and what you need. Each person should have the chance to share. Be respectful when others are speaking. Listen closely for points you have in common. When it is your turn, don't spend your time reacting to what was just said, instead, state your feelings and what you need.

Look for solutions that accommodate everyone involved. Look for what you have in common. Find creative ways to resolve the issue. Brainstorm solutions together staying detached from having to "win." You really only win when each of you feels the interchange has been successful.

Agree to evaluate the situation at a later date to determine if the solution is working. Keep the lines of communication open. Something may have been said during the conflict that still has you bristling. Check back again and ensure that the conflict was settled amicably.

Dealing with Criticism on the Job

Learning to be a valuable employee means you have to be willing to grow. Through constructive criticism, you can learn new skills and talents throughout your career. Although it may not be fun to take, without this criticism, you will remain exactly the same and not develop the skills you need for your career growth. Be careful not to interpret constructive criticism as a threat—you won't benefit if you are defensive.

> Mary Sue had worked in her job as an executive assistant for one year when her boss told her in a performance appraisal that she was slightly dogmatic. Even though her boss gave her an exceptional review, praised her accomplishments, and told her how much she was valued, Mary Sue couldn't get the one negative comment off her mind. She fretted about it for weeks. Several years later, Mary Sue admits that that comment was all she actually remembered word for word from her review and was still able to recall how it made her feel.

When you find yourself on the receiving end of criticism use these techniques:

- Listen to the criticism and consider it carefully before you speak. Resist the desire to defend yourself until you've heard all the details. For instance, if your supervisor snaps at your messy desk as she walks by, refrain from snapping back at her. Instead, recognize that your desk is probably out of hand, or that your boss is having a particularly difficult day.
- If you accept the criticism as true, say so. If you are unsure, take the time to think about it. Regularly repeated criticism from several unrelated parties is more likely to be valid.
- Ask for suggestions on how to change the criticized behavior. You could ask, "How would you handle this if you were in my place?"
- Before the conversation ends, summarize the criticism and your response to it. Repeat it back to the person who offered it. Make sure both of you understand the situation in the same way.
- If you feel the criticism is valid, plan a strategy for correcting the behavior. Think over what you have learned from the change.

Most businesses have built-in measures for giving you feedback on your performance, but performance appraisals don't just happen once or twice a year. Everyday you are being judged on your ability to perform the work in an effective manner. Although an appraisal of your performance on the job can be uncomfortable, if you follow the tips listed above, the appraisal will be all the more effective. But what happens if you disagree with the criticism?

Not all criticism is constructive or valid. If you feel the criticism is unjustified, you could listen to what the person has to say and then let it be known that you would like some time to think about what was said. Give a specific time and follow through on your agreement. When you meet, discuss why you disagree and support it with examples.

SUMMARY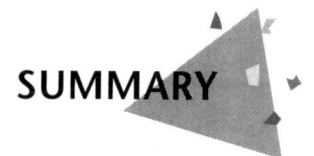

*To be a good communicator,
respect the opinions of others as well as your own,
listen for understanding, and work to find commonality.*

You can communicate through several mediums. In this chapter we dealt with verbal and nonverbal methods. It takes skill to effectively convey your message to others, and this skill can be continually developed. In addition to thinking before you speak, listening with an open mind, and communicating with respect for yourself and others, put yourself in the other person's position.

By developing good listening skills and nonverbal communication skills, you can be a better communicator. Stereotypes, prejudice, and discrimination are barriers to effective communication. Having good communication skills can help resolve conflicts. If conflict does exist, set ground rules, resolve the conflict when everyone involved is calm, take turns speaking, look for solutions that accommodate everyone, and evaluate the solution.

Applications & Exercises

5.1 What Is Your Communication Style?

Your unique communication style affects the things you say and how people perceive you. Although their perceptions may be incorrect, your communication style still makes an impact one way or another. In the following exercise, discuss some of your unique communication characteristics. Answer the list of questions. Once you have completed them, move into groups of three or four people. Each group should spend some time hearing each other's results. When everyone has had a turn, find out whether your group members had any common communication challenges and communication strengths. Discuss one communication challenge you all agree is the most difficult and then decide on an effective way to build strength in that area. When you are finished, share your ideas with the rest of the class.

Remember, there are no right or wrong answers, just different ways of communicating.

1. In a confrontation, I _____

2. I feel that public speaking is _____

3. It is difficult for me to talk about _____

4. If given a choice between writing and speaking, I prefer _____ because _____

5. In a group presentation, I usually _____

6. My greatest communication asset is _____

7. My biggest communication problem is _____

8. Whenever I listen to someone else talk, I really _____

9. I have a habit of _____ whenever I talk.

10. When I have something I really want to say, I might _____

11. I really dislike listening to lecturers who _____

12. My learning style affects my communication style in the following way:

5.2 Conflict Style Assessment

1. In a conflict I would rather retreat than fight. — Often   Sometimes   Never
2. In a conflict I am comfortable expressing my point of view. — Often   Sometimes   Never
3. I try to find ways for both people to win when I'm in an argument. — Often   Sometimes   Never
4. I prefer to walk away and cool down before I talk about the problem. — Often   Sometimes   Never
5. If I can't resolve a problem right away, I feel distraught until it's handled. — Often   Sometimes   Never
6. I usually need some time to process what I'm feeling and what is important to me. — Often   Sometimes   Never
7. If I can't resolve an issue, I agree to keep trying. — Often   Sometimes   Never
8. In a conflict, I would rather stick it out and resolve the issues right there and then. — Often   Sometimes   Never
9. More often than not, I am the one who initiates conflict. — Often   Sometimes   Never
10. If I can't resolve an issue, I agree to disagree and let it go at that. — Often   Sometimes   Never

Answer the following questions about your conflict style. If the class has time, share your patterns with another student.

1. Do you like how you respond in conflicts?

2. What would you change (if anything)?

3. What is your greatest strength during an argument?

4. What frustrates you most about the other person's behavior when you're in an argument?

5. How can you respond to the other person's conflict style when they are not acting as you'd like?

5.3 Nonverbal Communication

Divide into pairs and position yourselves so that you are facing one another. Each of you should think of something you want the other person to do. Take turns and try to convey what you want using only body language (gestures, nods, rolled eyes, etc.). Be sure and use no form of verbal or written communication whatsoever. Do not sigh, moan, or make any verbal sound. When one person has been successful, switch and do the exercise once more.

When both of you are finished, discuss whether this exercise was easy. Was the objective simple or complex? Was it accomplished? Why or why not? When everyone is finished, gather with the rest of the class and discuss your process.

WORKING TOGETHER

BODY LANGUAGE

In this exercise your class will need to divide into three different groups (unless the class decides to participate in all three assignments). Each group should choose a different exercise to complete.

- The first group should spend time looking through magazines to find different examples of nonverbal communication. When the group has a good-sized sample (10 or more), members should prepare a visual presentation for the rest of the class.
- The second group should put nonverbal communication to the test. Try standing closer or further away than you usually do in different types of conversations. Watch what happens to the listeners. Do they back up? Move closer? See what happens when your nonverbal communication doesn't match your spoken words. When your exercise is finished, prepare a presentation for the rest of the class. (Note—Be

respectful in this exercise. Don't intimidate or frighten anyone with your body language.)

- The third group will need to spend some time in the school hallway, at work, and in a casual setting to observe body language. Does body language change depending on the surroundings? What is different? What is the same? What unusual things did you observe? Prepare a presentation for the rest of the class on your findings.

CASE STUDIES

What Would You Do?

One

Your to-do list says you are to meet with Sam, one of your employees, to discuss his performance on a project. Sam is a good employee and you like him. You got to work early because you have to leave at noon for a series of important customer meetings. You have trouble getting your to-do list accomplished because of a number of interruptions. As a result, you are running behind and have only ten minutes to speak with Sam before you have to leave. That is a fraction of the time you have planned, but you decide to speak with Sam anyway. You focus on the key performance issues and efficiently communicate these. You feel like the meeting with Sam went well and you feel good that you got it done before you left. When you pick up your e-mail that evening at your hotel, you learn that Sam was very upset after your meeting. He did not feel like you wanted to hear his side of the story and work together to resolve the problem.

1. Was the goal to meet with Sam and take care of a to-do item or was there a more important goal?
2. Do you think Sam overreacted?
3. What is the reality of the workplace?
4. Is it so busy that bosses have very little time to sit down and interact?

Two

Your team is on a deadline to complete an engineering project. Because of the time constraints, you have asked your team to work on Sunday. Unfortunately, this has caused a conflict for John, one of your team members who is very religious. You decide to let John have Sunday off. Another team member, Roland, doesn't think it's fair that John gets the day off. Instead of dealing with his anger appropriately, he tells a joke about the Pope over the lunch table in front of John. John comes to you later in the day and complains about Roland. He tells you he is less concerned about the joke and more concerned about Roland's hostile behavior. He feels that the joke is a very good example of how Roland undermines him. You call Roland in to talk, and he tells you he feels badly about telling the joke and has already apologized, but

he thinks John is just too sensitive in general. You are very concerned because without a resolution to the conflict, the production of your team will suffer and the company could lose a very large contract.

1. What can you say to John and Roland to help them understand each other's point of view?
2. What specific steps would you take to resolve the issue?
3. List the steps you would take and why those steps are important to the situation's resolution.

Effective Workplace Reading

The Art of Interpreting and Understanding

KEY CONCEPTS
- How can you build your reading skills?
- How can you improve your retention of the material?

Reading is to the mind what exercise is to the body.

— Addison

Our society revolves around the written word. Although the growth of computer technology may seem to have made technical skills more important than reading skills, the focus on word processing and computer handling of documents has actually *increased* the need for employees who function at high levels of literacy.

Information, or more importantly, accurate information, is a primary element of any business organization. Everyday in the workplace you will need to scan documents for the key facts they hold, decipher whether the facts are correct, and respond to what you have read. The better you are at reading, the better able you will be at meeting the daily demands of your job. Although the majority of your reading work may be only one or two pages, your work may require you to read technical manuals, financial reports, budget reports, and so on. The following list is just a sample of documents you may need to read on the job.

Audit Report	Laboratory Report	Research Report
Compliance Report	Library Report	Research Study
Design Report	Manager's Report	Sales Report
Evaluation Report	Operations Report	Situational Report
Experiment Report	Periodic Report	Status Report
Feasibility Report	Production Report	Task Report
Incident Report	Progress Report	Test Report
Investigative Report	Proposals	Trip Report
Justification Report	Recommendations	Weekly Report

This chapter will help you become more adept at managing the enormous amount of written material you'll encounter at work. Because of the demands of your job, you'll need to know which information should be read thoroughly and which information can be scanned briefly for the key points. You will learn to question what you are reading, which will help you distinguish between important information and that which can be disregarded. Finally, you will learn how to become an active, proficient reader, retaining large amounts of material while at the same time categorizing what you have read according to priority. Lawyer Manuel Degas says:

> When I began my job as a first year lawyer, I wasn't prepared for the amount of time I would spend reading. Every day, file after file landed on my desk. By the end of my first week, I still had a stack of paperwork to read through. I knew that if I didn't get control of the situation, I'd be reading at nights and on weekends—not something I really wanted to do. Plus, I needed to stay on top of the work; people's lives depended on my doing a good job.

Manuel discovered in no short order that reading was a major part of his daily workload. So did Linda Wheeler when she began her job as the employee training supervisor in the human resource department of a software company.

Even though I had worked in the human resource department for five years, I wasn't prepared for the amount of paperwork and text I'd need to wade through in my new position as the training supervisor. Proposals from independent consultants arrived daily. Because I wanted to offer the employees the best training possible, I felt it was really important to thoroughly read each proposal. In addition, I needed to stay current on management theories—like the principles of chaos and change, web-structured organizations, and emotional intelligence—to name a few. My office began to look like a mini-library by the end of the first month on the job. I also read and reread every policy manual from our company, making sure we were complying with our standards. When I took the position, I thought I would spend more time interacting with the employees. Instead, I am spending the majority of my time reading. It's not what I had expected at all.

Even though Linda Wheeler has needed to spend a great deal of time reading at the onset of her new position, that probably won't always be true. In any job, there are ebbs and flows in the demands—especially when starting a new position. There are times when reading is not as crucial to your success on the job. Knowing the difference between the two—when to spend extra time reading and when to scan the information for key points—is a skill you will need to develop to be proficient on the job. Reading is a primary part of organizational life and workplace success, and this chapter is designed to help you develop this skill.

HOW CAN YOU IMPROVE YOUR READING SKILLS?

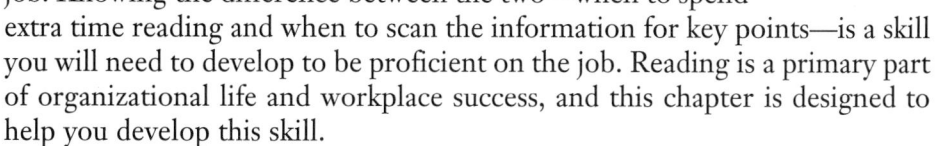

Some people seem to have a knack for retaining information with ease. Moreover, they are able to recall that information at a moment's notice. The more you use your brain to memorize and recall data, the better your brain becomes at memorization and recall. On the job you will pour through numerous documents, some lengthy and detailed and some short. Your ability to discern which information is pertinent and then recall that information when necessary will be a skill you'll need to develop and refine as you progress through your career.

Skimming and Scanning

Skimming and scanning are tools that can help you highlight the most important information in the quickest amount of time and that help you remember the dominant facts of what you read.

> **Skimming** is the rapid, superficial reading of material that involves glancing through to determine central ideas and main elements.

Scanning is reading material in an investigative way, searching for specific information.

Both skimming and scanning can be used when reading the same document. Consider how you might read an employee manual. You might *skim* the opening pages looking for the general flavor of the company values, such as in the mission statement, and the dedication the company has toward employees. From there you may *scan* for specific rules and regulations that must be adhered to in order to work in the company.

The same holds true for interoffice clippings, memos, and e-mail information. Don't waste valuable work time thoroughly reading each and every item that crosses your desk or lands on your computer. Instead, learn to evaluate its worth. Look at the end of e-mail documents to see if there is a summary. Look at the bulleted items in a memo. Discard clippings that may have been routed to every office but don't really pertain to your area. In short, learn to manage your reading.

Now try putting these two techniques to work. Read the following three paragraphs skimming the text for the central ideas. Your eyes should just glance through the entire paragraph at once. Don't try and read each and every sentence or word. When you are finished, answer the questions without looking back at the text, and see how well you were able to pick out the key points.

Cliched Corporate Conversations

You don't have to be a rocket scientist to recognize that corporate America is a leading-edge recycler of tired phrases. It's a no-brainer. Pitch artists swearing they walk the talk, bearing offers of win-win situations, are legion. But the bottom line is they don't want to be left out of the linguistic loop while colleagues who are a bit slower on the learning curve throw out slews of mouth-bitten cliches every time they touch base with you.

Our nation's bulging inventory of business cliches is spun out by pundits picked up by senior executives and regurgitated by pilot fish imitating their bosses. The explosion of management tomes and seminars in the past fifteen years has fostered a top-down commitment among business folk to pepper their vocabularies with the latest business jargon. As the pace of work becomes lightening quick, people condense complex historical events into flashy insights. "Just as reading diet books is a good substitute for losing weight, reading management books is a substitute for good management," comments Vanderbilt University Professor Terrence Deal.

In this age of cliches, meaninglessness reigns. Does anyone truly know what the "value chain" is? Or exactly what "empowerment" is? Avers Ralph Kilmann, professor at the University of Pittsburg's business school: "People feel comfortable with these concepts. They think they understand them because they use them in conversations, memos, and publicity statements, but there is virtually no substance to these words." Now that's vision!

Reprinted with permission, Erick Schonfeld, *Fortune*, copyright © Time Inc. All rights reserved.

QUESTIONS

1. What is the topic of the article? _____
2. What is the problem? _____
   _____
3. Is there a solution offered? _____

Next, read the following paragraph, but this time scan the information for important details. Again, look over the paragraph as quickly as you are able. Avoid reading word for word.

The Southwest Airlines Success Story

Southwest Airlines has been a remarkable airline success story. How did this happen? The company began 26 years ago, when two businessmen (its founders) were sitting in a airport dealing with the inconvenience of flying around the state of Texas. One took a napkin, wrote "Houston, Dallas, San Antonio" in three spots, and drew a triangle connecting the three city names. That triangle was the beginning of building an alternative to conventional air travel that would attract the public in droves. Southwest's owners decided to identify what would set their service apart from other airlines and then began promoting that uniqueness. Southwest takes as a given things like good customer service and on-time arrival and instead focuses on being interesting and down-home. In the process, Southwest has looked to its audience (people flying high frequency between cities and dealing with ever-changing schedules) and designed a business to meet the needs of its customers. Why provide inexpensive flights only for cross-continental travel to the largest cities? Southwest prides itself on "puddle-jumping"—offering flights to nearby cities for economical fares. Why give low prices for round-trip only? Southwest instituted the cheap one-way fare. Why limit service to Texas business people? When Southwest realized that its unique approach to air transportation was attractive to all kinds of people all over the country, it expanded its service. Southwest identified a need and filled a void. In short, Southwest made itself special.

From *Keys to Career Success* by Carter, Ozee, & Bollinger, © 1998. Reprinted by permission of Prentice-Hall, Inc., Upper Saddle River, NJ.

QUESTIONS

1. What is the main topic of the article? _____
2. What aspects of airline business does Southwest accept as a given? _____
   _____
3. What travel features does Southwest use to respond to their unique clientele? _____
   _____
4. Name the two qualities that describe Southwest's clientele. _____
   _____

Although you probably used the skimming and scanning methods frequently in your college life, it will be important to continue honing these skills. More than likely, you'll need to use them frequently in your work.

Use the SQ3R Approach

The term **SQ3R** stands for **S**urvey, **Q**uestion, **R**ead, **R**ecite, and **R**eview—all steps in an effective reading process. SQ3R not only helps you read more efficiently, it also helps you retain what you read. In business, you will want to be able to read reports and documents quickly and then accurately relay this information.

For instance, in one local department store chain, the CEO walks through the different store departments every morning asking each buyer and department manager questions about their department's productivity on the previous day. In order to give the CEO the requested information, the employees must have read the printouts from the previous day's activities. They would also have been required to memorize the figures so they could relay the information accurately.

S—Survey. If you are having trouble with a computer software program and go to the users manual to find a solution, what is the first thing that you might want to do with the manual? If you look it over to determine how it is laid out and the subjects it contains, you are using a form of surveying. When reading books, documents, or reports, surveying can help you understand the basic components of what you are reading. Surveying refers to the process of pre-reading the material before you actually read it in-depth. Most textbooks, books, and reports give the reader an overview of what is contained within. When you begin looking at new material, depending on the specific format, you could examine the following areas:

Text preface	Table of contents
Chapter summaries	End of text glossary
Text index	Text bibliography
Chapter titles	List of objectives
Chapter outlines	Opening stories
Major and minor headings	Special learning tools
Notes in the margins	**Bold** and *italicized* words
Tables and figures	Internal chapter progress checks
Photo illustrations	End of chapter key terms
End of chapter questions	End of chapter review

The easiest and most efficient way you can manage the surplus of reading found on the job is to begin with surveying. It gives you an idea of what you can expect in the document. For example, look at the following partial table of contents from *Leadership in Organizations* by Gary Yukl. (*Leadership in Organizations*, 4/e, by Yukl, © 1998. Reprinted by permission of Prentice-Hall, Inc., Upper Saddle River, NJ.)

Preface
I **Introduction: The Nature of Leadership**
　Definitions of Leadership
　Leadership Effectiveness
　Effective Leadership in Groups and Organizations
　Overview of Major Research Approaches
　Toward an Integrating Conceptual Framework
　Summary
　Review and Discussion Questions
II **The Nature of Managerial Work**
　Typical Activity Patterns in Managerial Work
　The Content of Managerial Work
　Theory of Demands, Constraints, and Choices

You'll notice when you scan the table of contents that the first chapter is primarily about the nature of leadership. You can assume that the chapter will thoroughly define leadership, how it is applied in organizations, and what research has been done in the field of organizational leadership. If you were to turn to the actual chapter and read the chapter heading and subheadings, you would gain further insight into the chapter's contents. Again, using Yukl's book on organizational leadership, you'll find the following headings and subheadings in Chapter I.

　Definitions of Leadership
　Leadership Effectiveness
　　Immediate and delayed outcomes
　　Direct and indirect effects
　　Causal chain of effects by leader (Figure 1–1)
　Effective Leadership in Groups and Organizations
　　Effective leadership in small groups
　　Effective leadership in open systems
　　Competing values
　　What criteria to use?

Q—Question. Your next step is to ask questions based on the survey you performed. These questions will focus your attention and increase your interest, helping you relate new ideas to what you already know and building your comprehension of the material. In the previous example, using the first heading in Yukl's table of contents, you could have asked questions such as:

HEADING	QUESTION
The Nature of Leadership	What is the nature of leadership?
	What are the aspects of leadership?
	Is leadership something that is part of the nature of mankind?

Can you provide questions for the rest of the headings?

HEADING	QUESTION
Definitions of Leadership	
Leadership Effectiveness	
Effective Leadership in Groups and Organizations	
Overview of Major Research Approaches	
Toward an Integrating Conceptual Framework	

The questions you ask give you a starting point for the reading, the first R in SQ3R. When you read the material with the questions in mind, you will be able to stay focused as you read. Read the material with the purpose of answering each question you raised.

R—Read. By reading actively you can become a better reader. To do this, you can ask yourself questions about the material as you are reading it.

Once you start to read, you'll notice right away if the material can be read quickly with few pauses or will need to be read at a slower pace. Frequently, material that is technical in nature will need to be read more slowly so that you can digest the data effectively. Besides altering your pace according to the degree of difficulty, the following tips can help you become a more proficient reader.

Get in the habit of marking the text after you read the document. If you mark text as you are reading you'll be prone to overmark. Wait until you've finished a section, then go back and highlight the key points.

Highlight key terms and concepts. Mark the examples that explain and support the important ideas. You might try using more than one highlighter color to differentiate definitions or ideas from examples.

Highlight figures and tables. Whatever information you need from the tables and figures should be highlighted along with any tables that summarize the concepts discussed in the text.

Write notes in the margin. Comments such as "main point" or "important definition" will help you locate key sections later on. In addition, note any questions you may have about the document's validity in the margins.

Be careful not to mistake highlighting for learning. You will not necessarily learn what you highlight unless you review it carefully. Be an active reader.

R—Recite & R—Review. Once you have asked yourself questions about the material you are reading, you may decide to recite the answers aloud. You could also discuss the topic about which you are reading with someone else, or you could write about the new information you have read in a notebook. Writing is one of the most effective methods to solidify what you've read. Use whatever techniques best suit your learning style profile. Finally, review what you have read to make sure you understand the material. Following are some tips for reviewing:

- Skim and reread your notes and then try summarizing from memory.
- Quiz yourself using the questions you initially raised in the Q stage.
- Create an outline of the material.
- Reread the tables, summary, preface, and headings.
- Recite important concepts to yourself.
- Think critically. Break ideas down into examples.

HOW CAN YOU IMPROVE YOUR RETENTION OF THE MATERIAL?

If you want to improve reading retention, practice the following guidelines.

Be Aware that Memory Is an Important Part of Your Job

Think how much more effective you will be if you can recall important facts without having to rifle through stacks of paperwork to look them up. When the CEO comes through your department and asks for the figures from yesterday's sales, think how efficient and impressive you will be if you can share the information from memory.

IN THE REAL WORLD: MERRILLYN SHROADS

> I grew up listening to dinner table discussions about retail—my whole family revolved around it. I guess you could say that it's in my blood.

Merrillyn Shroads came from a successful retail family, although she never really wanted to go into business. She was accustomed to the business talk of her enterprising father, and it was possibly for this reason that when Merrillyn graduated from the University of Wisconsin it was not with a degree in business, but history. "I felt the need to distance myself from everything that seemed so typical to me. I wanted to do my own thing, to test the waters, so to speak."

Upon graduation, Merrillyn got a job that required extensive travel. She was excited about this and applied herself wholeheartedly. The position provided a solid base on which a career could be built. Merrillyn enjoyed her transient lifestyle for a few years, but then found herself wishing for something closer to home. On a visit with her family one summer, her father suggested that she consider opening a branch of his kitchenware business in the city in which she was living. Merrillyn was hesitant, as she had no real business experience. However, the more she thought about it, the more she realized that this was not just an opportunity to be in business for herself, but also a wonderful way to be able to work with her father: "I thought that I should be making the attempt to learn as much as I could from him while I had him there to teach me."

Though she lived in another city, thousands of miles from her father, Merrillyn felt that she could receive the support she needed from him, and her store, Cook's Mart, was opened. She knew that she had no experience, but her desire to make it work led her to believe that it would. "My father's positive influence really helped me. He told me to have faith and be firm in the belief that nothing is impossible—that I have the ability to make things happen if I want them."

She knew that opening a retail business would be a risk, but she clung to her father's philosophy. She learned the business aspects as she went along, and her desire to make it work paid off. Cook's Mart was a success. She credits her willingness to learn something new as well as her support system for her success.

> I have been really lucky in that I have a wonderful support system, personally, in the form of my family; but I also have a wonderful support system, professionally, in the form of my staff. They are always working to put our best foot forward as a business. I think that this is apparent to our customers, and that it fosters in our customers a loyalty that many larger stores don't see.

Merrillyn feels that investigating and gaining a hands-on perspective of the profession that you want to pursue will help you develop a better sense of whether the profession is suitable for you. "I think that probably the most important characteristic you can possess is the ability to think positively and have the wherewithal to know that it can be done if you think it's possible."

Use a Mnemonic Device to Boost Your Memory Power

This device connects material you are trying to learn with other information that you already know. A song can be a mnemonic device. Acronyms are another type of mnemonic device, whereby you take the first letter of something you want to remember and turn it into a sentence. Physics instructors often supply the acronym "Roy G. Biv" to help students remember the colors of the spectrum. **Roy G. Biv** stands for **R**(ed), **O**(range), **Y**(ellow), **G**(reen), **B**(lue), **I**(ndigo), and **V**(iolet).

Retaining information is also made easier by grouping items together. When you have to remember lists of nonrelated information, break the information into pieces that you can manage.

Series of numbers can more easily be memorized . . .
7193031734   2027335022   4956693074
. . . when they are grouped into a phone number format
(719) 303-1734   (202) 733-5022   (495) 669-3074

Take Notes as You Read

When you read, jot down any information that you think is important. When you are finished reading, you should have a fairly decent outline of what you'll need to know or remember in the future. This way, you can refer back to your notes instead of having to reread the entire document.

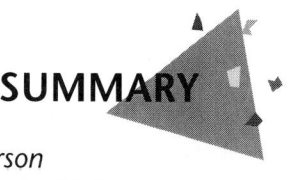

SUMMARY

The best way to become a successful business person is to read about a wide variety of subjects over the course of a lifetime.

To increase your reading effectiveness, use the following techniques:

- Survey the material.
- Turn the chapter headings into questions.
- Read the material, writing down important points.
- Separate the material into manageable sections.
- Recite aloud or write important points in a notebook.
- Review the material until you're sure you understand.
- Use mnemonic devices to help you remember.
- Practice, practice, practice.

Applications & Exercises

6.1 Applying Reading Techniques

This exercise gives you two different types of written material to read. One, a short memo, can be scanned fairly quickly. Remember, though, to highlight any points that may be important. The second paragraph, a more technical document, will take more time. You'll need to read more slowly, perhaps noting important points in the margins. After reading the two documents, move into small groups of three to five people and answer the questions that follow the selections. First answer the questions without looking back at the documents. How much were you able to retain? When you are finished, answer the questions one more time. This time, though, look back at the written material, especially your highlighted points and the notes in the margins. Was it easier? Did you highlight the key points? Which document was easier to understand and retain the information?

MEMORANDUM

Wahlscott Construction
West 232 Samson Avenue, Lee's Summit, Mo.
(816) 555-1425

To: Division Managers
From: Kaarin Moitoza
Subject: Division Meeting
Date: September 25, 1998

A meeting will take place on September 25th at 9:00 am in the west wing conference room. All division managers are required to attend.

The purpose of the meeting is to discuss the new HMO plan and how it will impact your employees. A representative from the HMO will give a detailed presentation of the plan followed by a period for questions. The meeting should take approximately two hours.

Each division manager should appoint a representative to relay the information to each department. The representatives will be responsible for holding briefings the week of September 28th. Your representative should also plan on attending the division meeting with you.

Any questions? Contact Beth Saunders at X-2245.

QUESTIONS CONCERNING THE MEMO

1. To whom is the memo directed? _____

2. What is the date, time, and length of the meeting? _____

3. What is the meeting about? _____

4. Who will be present at the meeting? _____

5. What follow-up action is required? _____

Consumer Interactions

The determination of consumer behavior is predicated upon two underlying conditions—the availability of income for expenditure (so-called disposable income) and the manner in which this available income is spent. To determine the amount of disposable income, the tax rate must be known, yielding a formula, $D = (Y - t)$, where D is disposable income, Y is total income, and t represents net taxes, here assumed at an average flat rate to avoid unnecessarily complicating the issue. In addition, it is necessary to know the value of the marginal propensity to consume (MPC), which is a measure of the tendency of the average person in the economy to spend a portion of the next dollar earned. A final necessary value is the amount of autonomous consumption in the society, that is, the minimum level of consumption that must take place for the population to survive. This factor is a discrete number based on historical data concerning prices and the level of consumption necessary for survival. It is usually represented as the constant a. Combining these factors, we find that the consumption function is described by the formula, $C = a + b \times (Y - t)$.

Social Issues in Technology: A Format for Investigation, 2/e by Paul A. Acorn, © 1997. Reprinted by permission of Prentice-Hall, Inc., Upper Saddle River, NJ.

QUESTIONS CONCERNING "CONSUMER INTERACTIONS"

1. Name the two underlying conditions that make consumer predictions possible. _____

2. What is $D = (Y - t)$? _____
3. What do the letters MPC stand for? _____
4. The definition of MPC is _____

5. Explain autonomous consumption. _____

6. The consumption function is represented by the formula _____

PERSONAL ASSETS

Your Reading Habits

Think about your reading skills. Do you read voraciously? Seldom? When reading difficult texts, do you find yourself reading the same paragraph over and over without really understanding what you've read? Do you like to read or do reading assignments pile up until you're forced to attend to them? Take some time and analyze your reading habits. Note your reading strengths and weaknesses and steps you will take to increase your reading abilities. When you are finished, share your reading habits with another person in class. In turn, listen to their reading habits.

WORKING TOGETHER

Memorization

For this exercise the class will need to divide into three different groups. After you have divided, your task will be to memorize the following information within a three-minute time frame. Each group will be asked to memorize using a different memorization technique. When the time is up, you'll need to *individually* write down your answers on a clean sheet of paper to see how well you did. Then try again, but this time allow everyone in your group to contribute to the answer.

PROCEDURE

1. Form groups.
2. Select a memorization technique and list to memorize.
3. Memorize the list.
4. After three minutes, individually write the list from memory.
5. Check your answer against the answers of other group members.
6. Refer to the original list and see how many you got right individually and as a group.
7. Discuss as a class.

SELECTION 1

Memorize the following list by saying the items out loud.

    Dual-in-line package
    Small outline integrated circuit
    Shrink small outline package
    Thin shrink small outline package

Thin very small outline package
Quad flat pack
Thin quad flat pack

SELECTION 2

Memorize the following list by writing it down over and over.

| .0342 | 1.998 | 665.02 | 621498.05 |
| .92 | 77.298 | 290.64 | 375551.44 |

SELECTION 3

Memorize the following list using an acronym you create as a group.

Altruistic, Humanitarian, Generous, Benevolent, Charitable, Kind, Humane, Giving, Caring, Good, Philanthropic, Compassionate

Documents
Communicating Through the Written Word

7

KEY CONCEPTS

- Why is good writing important to your success on the job?
- What should you do before you begin writing?
- What are the elements of good writing?
- What is the writing process?
- What documents are typically found in the workplace?

Whatever we conceive well, we express clearly.

Epictetus

114 CHAPTER 7   DOCUMENTS

ords, joined to form ideas, have tremendous power. Whether you are writing a memo, a formal report, or a letter of support or reprimand, your words carry powerful messages to the reader. How you convey yourself, either by going directly to the point or by taking the long and circuitous path to arrive at your point, invariably affects the reader's understanding of your message. Effective writing is a key component of a successful career. As you proceed through your career, you will need to be able to convey your ideas effectively. This chapter addresses how to use an efficient process to write in a clear and effective manner.

Consider the humorous memo below.

MEMORANDUM

TO: All Staff Members of Worde, Inc.

FROM: Denise Malapro
                    Vice President for Internal Communication

DATE: August 29, 1992

SUBJECT: Long Memos

The ability to develop effective internal communications is a crucial skill that we all should practice consistently. Concise, effective memos have always been a priority here at Worde. Indeed, I can safely say that our corporation has always been known for the quality of its sentence construction, since, as you would no doubt agree, overly long and complex sentences can confuse people and disguise meanings leading to misunderstandings on the part of the reader and certainly, frustration on the part of the writer, since his or her meaning has been misconstrued, whether partially or totally, to the point of almost complete obfuscation.

In a recent conversation with my staff, I learned that over 50 percent of our internal memos are more than five pages in length. Furthermore many of us use words that the average person just wouldn't use in normal conversation. This is simply heinous! This is why I am announcing a new company-wide policy. From now on, we will write only short, effective memos that get to the point quickly. It is time to be more aggressive about length control.

Contemporary Business Communication, by Boone et al., © 1994. Reprinted by permission of Prentice-Hall, Inc., Upper Saddle River, NJ.

Good writing reflects clear thinking and, indeed, depends upon it. Therefore, a clear thought process is the best preparation for a well-written document. Good writing also depends on reading. The more you expose yourself to the works of other writers, the more you will develop your ability to express yourself well. Not only will you learn more ideas, but you will learn more ways to put words together to express those ideas.

WHY IS GOOD WRITING IMPORTANT TO YOUR SUCCESS ON THE JOB?

The way we word our messages may sound fine to us, but in reality our words can have more than one meaning to the people who are interpreting what we write. Judy Blume, a writer of books for young adults, tells the story of a young girl on her first day of school. When she arrives the teacher greets her and then says, "Sit here for the present." Instead of understanding that the teacher was asking her to sit in one spot for the time being, the girl thought she was sitting there until her teacher brought her the present. Feeling great anticipation, she was afraid to move from her seat lest she miss her present.

Although her feelings may have been bruised, her misinterpretation of the words would probably not cause great harm. Not so, though, in the world of business. What you say or fail to say, and whether the information presented is accurate, can have a profound impact. Marvin Gates, a manager with an electronics firm, says his main gripe with new employees is that they don't know how to write.

> Even though they may have done quite well in school, most new employees fresh out of college don't even know how to write a standard business letter, let alone a month end report. And even when they do, the letters are frequently poorly devised. It usually takes a few months before the employees see that I'm really serious about well-written documents. It's not just for my benefit. They are representing the company as a whole. We can't afford to lose important clients because of poor grammar or incorrect spelling. It's important we put our best out into the marketplace.

Most people use the written word as a regular part of their business practice. Think how difficult a person's job might be if he or she could not persuade the customer to consider buying a certain product or service. The written word can actually tip the scales in the direction you want it to go if you learn to be an effective and persuasive writer. In the same vein, your words can actually cause you to lose a customer or a valued employee if you aren't paying attention to your word choices.

Although you may believe that you are being tactful, to another you may sound overly solicitous or condescending. While you may think your letter has a friendly tone, to someone else it may come off as too "chatty" or unprofessional. Even though it is highly unlikely that you will be able to please everyone, at least take the time to analyze your writing for tone quality and accuracy of information to see if it conveys the meaning you had in mind.

Your writing will be much more effective if you remember the following:

- Words are interpreted—they mean different things to different people.
- Words can trigger emotional responses.
- Words can carry hidden messages and meanings.
- The words you choose reflect how you see the world.

- Words can uplift as well as defeat.
- Sometimes words cannot express what you want to or mean to say.

Words Have Power

One reason good writing is so important on the job is because of the power of language. The messages that you convey, whether written or spoken, are composed of both content and form. The following tips can help you keep the tone of your words positive and professional:

- When you disagree with another's point, instead of saying "You're wrong about . . ." say, "even though you said such and such, another way to look at it is . . ."
- When you want to bring home a certain point, instead of saying "Let me make this perfectly clear . . ." say, "Again, I would like to point out how important this is . . ."
- When you want someone to agree with you, instead of saying "everyone I know already agrees that . . ." say, "I hope you can see the validity in my point . . ."
- When you're hurt by another's behavior, instead of saying, "Are you happy now?" say "I'm hurt by what you just said."

Now it's your turn. Rephrase the following statements.

1. That's the way we do things around here!

2. I don't care. That's the way it's gonna be.

3. No one said it was going to be easy.

4. That's nothing—you should hear about the time . . .

5. Don't worry about me, I'll just . . .

Words Trigger Emotions

Words, both written and spoken, can trigger emotions. Knowing which words to use can save you from communication blunders. Using "you" statements, for example, can offend some people and trigger strong emotions in the reader. Practice using words that are inclusive, kind, positive, and appropriate to the situation. Avoid using words or phrases such as:

"You" statements:	"You never let me . . ."
	"Why don't you . . ."
	"How come you always . . ."
Gender-biased:	Use titles such as police officer instead of policeman.
	Use chairperson instead of chairman.
Blanket statements:	"Everyone feels this way."
	"You never do your share of the work."

Words Can Have Different Meanings

People assign meaning to words. Just as there are many different types of people, there are many different meanings that can be assigned to a particular word or phrase. Remembering this point will save you frustration when your coworkers or friends misinterpret your messages. To avoid misinterpretation, try the following:

- Ask for feedback.
- Avoid using either/or statements that polarize the reader.
- Make sure your choice of words is politically correct.
- Use examples that illustrate what you mean.
- Make sure the document is written on clean, fresh paper. Sending an apology on wrinkled or torn paper, for example, may say a great deal about your sincerity.
- If you want to emphasize a point, do so by using words to convey your thoughts. Refrain from "shouting" by using all capital letters or adding several exclamation points.

WHAT SHOULD YOU DO BEFORE YOU BEGIN WRITING?

Most often, in business, you will either be writing to *inform* or writing to *persuade*. If you want your employees to know about the new employee manual, use an informative style. On the other hand, if you want to make sure your employees read the new manual, use a persuasive tone when you write your memo. Every writing situation is different, and your goal is to understand each element before you begin to write.

State Your Purpose

Writing without stating a purpose is like driving without directions; you'll get somewhere, but maybe not where you needed to go. Whenever you prepare to send a memo or write a formal report or letter, spend a few moments thinking about what you want to accomplish. What is the end goal?

What do you want to accomplish with this particular piece of writing? State your purpose up front so readers have a frame of reference for interpreting the document.

Analyze Your Audience

Who will read your writing? In almost every case, a writer creates written material for work so that it can be read by others. The two parties in this process are the writers and their audience. Knowing who your audience is will help you communicate successfully. Ask yourself the following questions about your audience:

What are my readers' experiences? What type of background will the readers have? What are their interests and goals? What motivates them? Can you be direct or do you need to soften what you're saying? How might they react?

What are their roles? Are they supervisors, clientele, coworkers, contractors, or employees? Monitor the tone you take in your letters and reports. Are you too casual? Overly formal? Have you addressed them according to their preferences? Before you send documents, spend a few minutes looking at how you are addressing your audience.

How much do they know about the topic? Are they experts in the field or beginners? Are they highly technical people who need little or no explanation or do they need step-by-step instructions? Do they have expertise in what you're writing about or not?

What do I need from them? Am I asking my audience to change something? To get back to me? To follow through on something? What do I want them to think or do?

What is the writing protocol for their company? Each company approaches written material in its own unique way. Look at whether important messages are typed or hand written. Notice whether titles or first names only are used. Are letters summarized at the beginning or the end of the letter? Decide if you should follow the same or similar protocol.

Organize the Content

One of your writing goals is to organize the material in such a way that your readers can follow your train of thought. Suppose, for example, that you are writing an informative paper for a nonexpert audience on using on-line services. One way to accomplish your goal is to begin by explaining what these services are and the kind of help they can offer the user. Then, describe each service in detail and end with how these services are changing the face of the marketplace in the twenty-first century.

Look over the following memo and locate the purpose, topic, and audience to whom the memo is written.

> # MEMORANDUM
>
> TO: Patrice Roberts, Supervisor
> FROM: Albert Finnigan, Manager
> DATE: October 2, 1999
> SUBJECT: Conference
>
> Please contact the appropriate people in your hotel for the following needs for the upcoming conference. First, we will need an assortment of entree items to choose from. Since we have both vegetarian and nonvegetarian clientele coming to this conference, we'll need suggestions from both categories. Secondly, we will need the specifics on your different hotel accommodation packages. What types of rooms are available? Do you have pictures we can send the conference attendees? We will also need transportation specifics (airport shuttles, car rentals, shuttles to Disneyland). Finally, we are hoping you include passes to the amusement parks and local golf courses. Could you please send the specifics?
>
>   Thanks for taking care of this.

WHAT ARE THE ELEMENTS OF THE WRITING PROCESS?

After surviving college, most of you probably already know the basic elements of writing an effective paper. Nevertheless, the following information can be used as a review and a chance to continue honing your writing skills—skills that will come in handy in the workplace.

Develop a Plan

Think about what you're going to write and how you want to write it. The following guidelines will get the process started.

Brainstorm ideas and then narrow your ideas down to the most relevant.

Try *freewriting* to generate ideas. When you freewrite, you write whatever comes to mind about the topic without censoring your ideas or worrying about grammar, spelling, or punctuation. Freewriting helps you think creatively and gives you the opportunity to process your ideas and thoughts in a visible form. Sometimes, especially when the topic is a difficult one like formally reprimanding behavior or turning someone down for a promotion, freewriting can help you find just the right words and tone.

Ask *journalistic questions*. *Who* needs this information? *What* am I trying to get across in my letter/report/memo? *When* does this need to be accomplished? *Where* is the event/meeting being held? *Why* is this meeting/information so important? *How* can the information in the report be conveyed with accuracy and readability?

Make a *working outline*. The final step in the preparation process involves writing a working outline. Use this outline as a loose guide instead of a finalized structure. As you draft your document, your ideas and structure may change several times. Only by allowing changes can you be sure that your document reflects what you want.

Develop a Draft

A draft is imperfect—in grammar, style, word choice, spelling, punctuation, and organization. When drafting a document, the only concern should be on idea formation. You can fix the errors later. Begin by freewriting your draft. At this point don't think about your introduction, conclusion, or structure within the body of the document. Focus on getting your ideas out of the realm of thought and onto paper. Once you have the beginning of a paper in your hands, you can begin to refine it.

First, you'll need to write an **introduction.** The introduction tells your readers what the rest of the paper will contain. Include the premise or point of the letter or document in the first couple of paragraphs.

You'll also want to have a **hook**—something that grabs the reader's attention right off the bat. You can use an anecdote, a relevant quote, dramatic statistics, or a question that encourages critical thinking on the part of the reader. For example, if you are enticing a client to sign up long-distance customers, you could begin with . . .

What do Telecon, the rain forest, and your customers have in common? More than you think. Right now, every new client who signs up for Telecon's long distance service will have a tree planted in the rain forest in Brazil. That's right! Not only will . . .

Next you'll need to create the **body of the paper, report,** or **letter.** In this section you develop the main idea by giving examples that support your central theme. Examples should be arranged in an orderly fashion making it easier for the reader to stay focused on what you're saying. You can arrange your ideas in many ways, by time, for example, or according to importance. Ask yourself if you have met the criteria for the paper. Have you supported your ideas with fact? Have you developed ideas in a logical fashion?

Finally, you'll need to write your **conclusion.** The conclusion provides closure for the document. Aim to summarize the information found in the body of the paper, as well as to critically evaluate what is important about the information. You can use one of the following techniques:

- A summary of main points
- A quote, story, or question
- A request of the reader

Revise

When you revise, you **critically evaluate** the word choice, paragraph structure, and style of your first draft. Any draft, no matter how good, can always be improved. Try not to revise too much, though. Some people keep revising until they have an entirely different paper including a different thesis statement. Revise until you're sure your report or document flows smoothly, says what you mean, and is organized so that it is easy to understand.

Ask yourself:

- Is my document easy to understand?
- Have I stated and developed my thesis statement effectively?
- Do I use logical transitions as I connect ideas together?
- Is my writing style clear and concise?
- Does the introduction capture the reader's attention?
- Does the conclusion offer a natural ending to the paper?

Edit

At this point, you can edit your work. Begin by reading it aloud or having a friend read it aloud for you. If you stumble over the words or certain phrases, check to make sure they are well written. Correct technical mistakes such as spelling, grammar, punctuation, and faults in style consistency that occur, for example, in abbreviations and capitalizations.

Look for sexist language that might characterize people based on their gender. Sexist language often involves pronouns like "he" or "his." Use plural construction whenever possible to avoid the problem. You can use "s/he" as a solution in some cases. Or, alternate use of "he" and "she" in examples.

If you can, have someone check your work. Turning in a report that has misspellings or mistakes in grammar says a lot about you to the reader. Use the spell checker on your computer. Your written word makes an impression—make it a positive one.

WHAT DOCUMENTS ARE TYPICALLY FOUND IN THE WORKPLACE?

This section discusses the various types of business documents that are used in today's workplace. Familiarize yourself with each one, noting the rules for formatting, and any etiquette requirements. In this fast-paced world of work, there is a trend towards minimizing the amount of written work. The fast pace, though, has also increased the numbers of errors in paperwork. Although speed is increasingly important, speed does not negate the need for proper grammar, spelling, and a good basic structure. Use complete sentences and refrain from using bullets too frequently. They can be a disguise for undeveloped ideas and thinking. Make sure your letters, memos, and documents reflect your professionalism. It will make a marked difference in how you are perceived.

Business Letters

You will probably write hundreds of business letters in your professional careers. Although some of you may have assistants to take care of the business letters, learn to write them yourself so that you are informed enough to teach your staff. A business letter contains the following features.

Letterhead. Although most businesses use letterhead stationary, if yours doesn't you'll need to type the name of the person sending the letter and his or her address.

The date. The date line should be at the left margin beneath the letterhead. The date should reflect the day and year that the letter was written. Refrain from using all numbers for the date. Instead write out the month, followed by the day and year. The date on a letter should follow this format:

January 9, 1999

The inside address. The address of the person to whom you are sending the letter should follow the date. Write the name of the person followed by his or her title. Then add the company name and the complete address of the company. Your inside address should look something like the following:

Marion Sumner, Vice President
Sumner Logging and Timber
2121 West Woodglen Road
Astoria, OR 44651

The salutation. The salutation line offers a personal greeting to the recipient of the letter. Generally, you would write "Dear" followed by "Mr., Mrs., or Ms." After that you would add the reader's surname (last name) followed by a colon. It should look like the following:

Dear Mr. Thompson:

Sometimes you will be unable to add the name of the person to whom the letter will be read. In such case, it is acceptable to leave out the salutation line and begin with the body of the letter.

In addition, there will be times when you will not be able to tell the gender of the reader by looking at the name. If this is the case, write the first and last name for the greeting or leave out the salutation line altogether.

The body. The body of the letter should be well-written using the techniques listed previously in the chapter. Center the body of the letter, making sure that there is plenty of white space on all sides.

The close. The close is a one or two word formal goodbye. Closes such as Sincerely, Yours truly, Respectfully, or With warm regards can be used to close the letter.

The signature. There are a few different ways you can close your letter. You have the option of your name (typed) with your title directly underneath. Between the closing and your typed name and title, leave a block of space so you can hand write your name when the letter is finished. You may also want to add the name of the company. In that case, type it directly under the closing and proceed as previously suggested.

Sincerely,	Sincerely,
	Wells Fargo Bank
Kaitlin McGrew	Kaitlin McGrew
Director of Finance	Director of Finance

Initials and enclosures. The initials inform the reader who typed the letter and who composed it. The initials are typed two lines below the signature block. The writer's initials come first followed by the typist's initials.

DB/jp or DB:jp

If you are going to include an enclosure in the envelope, type "Enclosure" below the initials, or "Enc."

Memos

Memos are documents that usually appear within an organization. Short for memorandum, the memo is less formal than a business letter. Because you most likely already know the writer, less time needs to be spent building a rapport with the reader. Also, memos are shorter in length and more to the point—usually containing only one theme. Memos are constructed in the following manner:

MEMO

To:	[the person who will receive the memo]
From:	[the person writing the memo and initialed by that person]
Date:	[the day, month, and year the memo was written]
Subject:	[the theme of the memo]
	[The body of the memo]
	[No signature is necessary]

E-Mail

The e-mail system is quickly becoming the preferred method of communication in business. Instead of making a phone call or typing a letter, you can lay out your thoughts on your computer, hit SEND, and off it goes. The advantages of e-mail are numerous. There is a trend for using abbreviations and less formality, making e-mail time-efficient. Recipients can read their e-mail three or four times a day and respond when they have available time. This saves you from interruptions by phone calls and having to break your train of thought while you're working on important projects.

There is also a down-side to e-mail. Your mail will not be private. In fact, your mail can easily be accessed by millions of people. Because your mail can stay in your computer's backup system for years, be careful what you say. It may come back to haunt you at a later date.

Following are some tips for using e-mail.

Send only company messages on your business e-mail. Avoid the temptation to communicate with family and friends while at work. Personal e-mail can take a lot of time out of your day.

Don't send letters when you're angry or use all capitals to show that you're shouting. Wait until you've thought through your feelings before jumping to send it over the e-mail system. It's impossible to take back once you've sent it. Delay your impulse to react.

Be careful when using jokes or sarcasm. It is wise to limit jokes and sarcasm in e-mail because they are often misinterpreted by the reader.

Don't write anything you want to keep private. Sensitive company information should not be sent over the e-mail. Refrain from gossiping or berating another person for their actions. E-mail provides little privacy.

Scheduled Reports

Monthly or weekly reports can be wonderful tools for keeping people informed of the progress you are making as well as helping you stay focused on your accomplishments each month. Although reports can greatly vary depending on their purpose, they might include the following components and subjects.

Objectives. Usually a month-end report will address the objectives for the month and whether these objectives were accomplished along with how well they were accomplished.

Budget. You may discuss the overall budget for your department, spending to date, and the remaining amount of available budget.

Sales. You may also discuss the gross sales for your department along with the projected and actual sales. In addition, you may discuss sales to date.

Projects. Be sure to keep your employers informed about ideas you have for projects and the status of current projects.

Personnel. If you have people working for you, you may need to discuss their performances, any additional training they may need, whether you need more employees, or whether you are considering letting someone go.

Problems. You may need to discuss any conditions with which your employers should be aware. Alert them to conditions that will impact the company—customers that are thinking of removing their accounts, changes in the company systems that impact performances, and so on. Provide possible solutions along with the concern.

Competition. Discuss any changes in the marketplace and countermeasures you recommend or have taken. Compare your performance against the performance of competitors. Discuss what changes need to be made to enhance performance levels.

SUMMARY

Your words carry great power—choose them with care.

Even though you may have excelled at writing while in high school, you probably were surprised at how different the writing demands were once you entered college. The same is true of the change in writing expectations from college to the workplace. The writing standards will be higher. When you begin your first job, pay attention to the writing culture. Note how others address memos and e-mail. It can take time to adjust to a new way of conveying your ideas. Sometimes your employer will ask you to resubmit your work. That's okay. Learn from the experience.

Lynn Troyka, author of *Quick Access*, a reference book for writers, writes: "Many people assume that a real writer can magically write a finished product, word by perfect word. Experienced writers know that writing is a process, a series of activities that start the moment they begin thinking about a topic and end when they complete a final draft." Continue developing your writing skills. Your written word carries great power and is an important key to your workplace success.

IN THE REAL WORLD: ROBERT POND

"Learning is life."

Bob Pond developed this philosophy early in his life and still holds firmly to it today. Currently a professor emeritus at Central Ohio Technical College, Bob credits the success in his career to his motivation to challenge his abilities and to his grandfather who instilled in him the desire to learn as much as possible from the world around him. "He was an excellent role model—he read the classics and thought a great deal about the humanities, even though he only had an eighth grade education."

After high school, Bob entered the Air Force where he worked in the electronics division. This position introduced him to people who were educated in the field, and they fostered his desire to seek a degree. After completing four years in the military, Bob decided to pursue his degree. He attended a small liberal arts college full-time, while also working full-time to support himself. Before he completed his degree, he was offered a position in civil service working on missile and aircraft inertial guidance systems, where he became more confident in his abilities.

During this time, Bob also finished his education, obtaining a bachelor of science degree from Ohio State University. Completing his education worked to his benefit, enabling him to be promoted many times. Upon leaving his civil service post, Bob was hired as an instructor in engineering technologies at a local technical college. "I was thrilled with my position, felt challenged as never before, and enjoyed working with students, doing experiments in the laboratory, and simply being in an intense learning environment for myself and the students."

It was during his years as an instructor that Bob returned to college to obtain his master's degree. After five years as an instructor at Central Ohio Technical College, Bob was made chairman of their engineering technologies division.

He served eight years as chairman before making the decision to return to the classroom—his "first love." He has rounded out his career by writing technology textbooks. Now retired, he still teaches occasionally.

> My college education prepared me to confront challenges confidently, to help others to achieve their goals, and to serve my community. I have benefited immeasurably with a comfortable retirement and, hopefully, many more years of writing and sharing with others in our world.

CHAPTER 7 DOCUMENTS **127**

Applications & Exercises

 Freewriting

Imagine you are being asked to write a summary of your accomplishments for a monetary award. What would you say about yourself? Write what comes to your mind now.

 Drafting a Letter of Acceptance

Using the writing techniques from the chapter, draft a letter of acceptance to the company of your choice. Be sure and have an opening paragraph, a paragraph that develops your points, and a paragraph that sums up your letter.

 Editing Your Work

Read the following memo and then check it for errors. When you are finished, rewrite the document with another student in a more professional manner using the techniques you previously learned. Look at:

Content: Does the memo effectively say what was intended? How do you know? Does the memo grab your attention? Are you more likely to read the memo in its entirety or would you skim it?

Grammar: Has the writer used grammar that is accurate and effective? What would you recommend instead, if anything? Are the word choices the best ones? Why or why not?

Spelling: Has the writer checked for accuracy?

Tone: Does the memo sound inviting, threatening, condescending, or placating? Does it have the right tone for the message being conveyed? Why or why not?

MEMORANDUM

TO: Mike Baldwin
FROM: Annette Goosen
DATE: July 15, 1999
SUBJECT: Team Leaders Meeting

As you are most certainly aware, I have established a team leaders meeting in this time yearly. I have already heard back from John and Saarai. John and Saarai is both coming. Unfortunately, they cannot attend on the date I selected so we'll have to find a date that works for all. Both Sarrai and John are not hear on Tuesdays. In addition, tomas did agree to come. We were wondering if you will be there to help us with our fall projections. It would certainly help us formulate our ideas for the fall season. You are particularly crafted in ocming up with innovations.

   Please get back to me as soon as you can. I look forward to your reply.

PERSONAL ASSETS

Your Writing Skills

How well do you write? Look back at some of your recent writing, business letters, reports, or papers from college and assess your writing skills. In order to improve, what steps will you take?

1. What would you like to change about the way you write?

2. What do you like best about your writing?

3. What steps have you made or are you going to make to improve your writing skills?

4. Do you regularly work on increasing your vocabulary? How? Or why not?

5. When you receive mail, memos, documents, or reports, what do you like best about the writing style? What do you least like?

6. Do you regularly read other people's works? Reading increases your writing skills. What steps will you take to read more?

WORKING TOGETHER

Editing

For this exercise the class will need to divide into four different small groups. Each group needs to write a one-page monthly report using the format described earlier in the chapter. When you are finished, you will hand your paper over to another group for editing. Be sure to include plenty of mistakes in your letter. You can have:

- Spelling errors
- Errors in grammar
- Errors in punctuation
- Gender bias or sexist language
- Incorrect formats

After you have written your letter and edited another group's letter (if there is time), rework your letter until it is free from error.

CASE STUDIES

What Would You Do?

Look at the following memo to see if you can come up with a more effective tone so that the recipient does not feel offended or put off. How can you get the same point across without shaming the recipient? Which words are offensive? After you respond to the questions, gather in groups and rewrite the letter using a different, more professional tone.

MEMORANDUM

TO: David Brown
FROM: John Barker
DATE: December 10, 1998
SUBJECT: Company Policy

Yesterday, your behavior at the Christmas party was completely unacceptable. Even though it was a party after regular office hours, I can't condone what you did. Drinking in excess, leering at the president's wife, and making a general fool of yourself was completely disgusting. Due to your belligerent behavior, we have now lost the right to hold parties at the Harrison Resort. I am appalled and embarrassed to call you a colleague.

    Let me make it perfectly clear when I tell you that you have jeopardized your position in this company. I hope you learn your lesson well . . . and quickly.

QUESTIONS

1. Which words in the memo caused you discomfort?

2. If the writer was David's supervisor would the tone be different than if the writer was David's equal? How so?

3. If a friend of yours had received this memo, what would you recommend they do in response?

4. Revise the memo.

Two

Nathan is extremely angry with another salesperson. Last week Nathan received a call from one of his regular advertisers telling him that another salesperson had called on him trying to solicit his business. Nathan was furious. He worked alongside this salesperson every day. In fact, their desks were near enough that he could almost reach across the space and answer the other's phone. Even though there was no written policy on stealing accounts, there certainly was an unspoken agreement between the sales staff. Bart was new, though. He was aggressive and able to land accounts that others had tried to get for years. Nathan knew he would have to handle the situation with some delicacy. His boss really liked Bart's work. Nathan didn't want to jeopardize his own position just because he was mad at Bart.

Draft a memo to Bart. When you are finished, form small groups and discuss each other's memos. Which memo or sentences say it best? Why? After your discussion, as a group, rewrite the memo and then share your final product with the entire class.

Teamwork and Leadership

Working Effectively with Others

KEY CONCEPTS

- Why are good relationships essential to your success?
- How can you participate effectively as a member of a group?
- What are leadership qualities?

> Never doubt that a small group of thoughtful, committed people can change the world. Indeed, it is the only thing that ever has.
>
> Margaret Mead

Many times, groups are formed out of a need to accomplish a certain goal. In business, the goal could be as simple as planning the holiday party or as complex as designing a new product line. Sometimes the whole can be worth more than the sum of its parts—a group working together can accomplish more, and produce a better result, than would result if each individual was working alone. When individuals come together, though, this can create problems. We begin to struggle over who is right, who gets to lead, and which steps we're going to follow to accomplish our goals. We fuss over how others contribute and whether they're contributing enough. We form alliances, succumb to "group think," withhold from the rest of the group, or try to manipulate events to accomplish our personal agendas. That's the bad news.

The good news is that we can grapple with difficult issues and learn to work through them. We can listen to and learn from the ideas other group members bring to the table. We can support one another and carry more than our share when another group member needs help. We feel connected and a part of something greater than ourselves. We become invested in the success of our peers and the larger company as a whole.

When groups form to work collectively on a project, leaders emerge who can take charge and guide the group toward accomplishing a specific goal. Even though every person in a group may have the potential to lead, not everyone feels comfortable acting in the leadership role. Some organizational researchers theorize that leaders are born with innate leadership qualities, while other researchers insist that leadership is a skill that can and should be developed. Not everyone wants to lead, though. Leading can be a perilous business. It means sticking your neck out and fighting for solutions in the face of obstacles. It can also mean being unpopular with some people because you hold to what you feel is best for the group's goals, which is not necessarily what makes everyone happy. Even though you may be uncomfortable leading, to get ahead in today's workplace you will probably need to develop leadership skills.

Mark Norton, a manager for a plastic manufacturing company, says: "You wouldn't believe how many people come to us wanting management positions with little or no evidence of leadership skills. When a person applies, I look for how well they listen, if they can ask pertinent questions about the position, how thoughtful they are about answering the questions, and what kinds of successful leadership experiences they have had in the past. People should take the time to know their leadership strengths and work at developing what they don't have."

When you work in groups or lead others, your ability to effectively communicate will be crucial to your success. This chapter will help you understand how you can work effectively within groups and how you can develop leadership skills.

WHY ARE GOOD RELATIONSHIPS ESSENTIAL TO YOUR SUCCESS?

Margaret Wheatley, author of *Leadership and the New Science*, researched the nature of change within the universe using quantum physics. She then applied her findings to organizations. Today, Wheatley is a much sought-after consultant because of her expertise in helping organizations find solutions for the internal problems they face. She says:

> In the quantum world, relationships are not just interesting; to many physicists, they are all there is to reality. We do not exist in a vacuum. All things interact with each other. Successful human interaction is an essential part of your pathway to career success. With relationships, we give up predictability for potentials. Several years ago, I read that elementary particles were "bundles of potentiality." I have begun to think of all of us that way, for surely we are as undefinable, unanalyzable, and as bundled with potential as anything in the universe. None of us exists independent of our relationships with others. Different settings and people evoke some qualities from us and leave others dormant. In each of these relationships, we are different, new in some way.

If Wheatley's observations are correct, relationships are perhaps the most important element in our work life. Indeed, relationships and teamwork are vital to the success of an organization. The relationships we have with others in a team and how we "see" them can, like a self-fulfilling prophecy, determine the group's potential. Relationships also

- Provide a greater ability to solve problems.
- Offer rich and diverse ideas.
- Give emotional support.
- Spark creativity and innovations.

HOW CAN YOU PARTICIPATE EFFECTIVELY AS A MEMBER OF A GROUP?

As an employee, becoming aware of the group process and learning to respond to the unique attributes that arise can help you be a more effective team player. If you knew ahead of time that chaos and change are a natural part of a group's development, conflicts wouldn't catch you by surprise. Instead, you would be able to meet an uncomfortable moment with the knowledge that it was, perhaps, necessary to accomplishing your group's objectives.

> "In school, I always hated group work," says Maryanne Heinemann. "It was uncomfortable moving our desks in a circle and being forced to learn about one another. One or two people would invariably lead the discussion while the rest of us waited until we were asked to participate. I always felt uncertain at the beginning. After I got to know the people and figured what role they were going to take in the group, I felt much better—safer somehow."

While some people feel uncertain at the beginning of group work, others dive in with gusto. How you greet and get to know the others within your group can depend a great deal on your learning style. If you're an introspective learner, you might prefer to wait awhile before you begin to participate. If you're a visual learner, watching other people's interactions would be important for you. People who process verbally may tend to dive right in and say what is on their minds.

Like any new experience, at the beginning you might feel uncertain. Because the situation is unfamiliar to you, until you've settled in and found your bearings (your role within the whole), you might be hesitant to share who you really are and the ideas that motivate you. Being personable and professional are the best suggestions for a successful beginning. But what does personable and professional actually mean?

Speak Up When It's Important

When you actively listen to the input of others, you can hear when the discussion warrants your comments. Listen for problems to be solved, timelines to be addressed, creative contributions that need to be added, or work assignments that need to be made. Learn to listen carefully and speak up when you have an important contribution.

Develop Your Creative Thinking Skills

Some people naturally thrive on using their creative minds. When these individuals work together, it is as if they "feed" off of one another. They create much more together than they could alone. Learn to join in on the creative process. The benefits to your company are enormous.

Offer Suggestions, but Try Not to Be Invested in Them

The creative process can begin with a group brainstorming ideas until a solution is found. Many of your ideas and the ideas of the other group members will be discarded in the process. Try not to be attached to your contributions. They spark ideas in others, allowing the end result to be accomplished. If you really think your idea is the best solution, speak up again and provide reasons for why you feel the way you do.

Be Discreet

Occasionally, situations in your personal life arise that can impact the work you are doing. You can share your challenges without going into personal details by letting the group know that a family concern or a health concern is causing some additional stress. It is not necessary to share the details of your struggles—save that for close friends. Instead, divulge enough to let others know why you may not be at your best that day. Then move on to the work at hand.

Avoid "Group Think"

Nothing stifles creativity like "group think," which happens when the participants of a group stifle their own basic philosophies or ideas in order to reach a consensus. You can avoid this by using your critical thinking skills and speaking up when you have differing ideas. More than likely, by speaking your opinions, you will help others feel more comfortable in doing the same.

Group Conflict

Invariably, when groups come together to accomplish a goal, conflict occurs. Although many of us would rather not deal with conflict, it can actually have a positive effect on the group's end goals. In fact, some researchers suggest that conflict is a natural and orderly phenomenon that must occur before the change or goal can happen. Margaret Wheatley says this of conflict and chaos:

> The things we fear most in organizations—fluctuations, disturbances, imbalances—need not be signs of an impending disorder that will destroy us. Instead, fluctuations are the primary source of creativity.

Group activities can foster all kinds of conflict—frustration at a team member who always comes late or unprepared, annoyance at a member who always has to leave the meeting every half an hour for a cigarette, or agitation with a member who always seems to control the proceedings. Conflict can be as simple as arguing over whether the window should be open or can be as complex as making a decision about which medical plan the company should adopt. How you resolve conflict can mean the difference between a full-scale war and a general skirmish. Learn the rules of conflict and use them whenever it arises in your work.

Develop a plan for managing conflict. Even before your group experiences any disturbances, talk about effective ways to manage conflict; that way there will be some ground rules on which you can all rely. Discussing it beforehand makes it easier to manage later on. For instance, you can decide on how you want conflict expressed, whether personal attacks are forbidden, whether conflict needs to be resolved immediately or whether it can wait a few days.

Watch for signs of conflict. You can usually see conflict coming. A person may physically bristle when someone else speaks. Watch people's body language during discussions; it will give you a clue as to their feelings. Also note seating preferences, nonverbal clues, and whispered comments. When you see them, ask the person to express what is going on for them. Allow people to express any contrary feelings they may have during your group meetings.

Agree to respect differing opinions. Not everyone in your group is going to agree all the time. Allow others to voice their opinions even when you don't agree. Try and see the value in what they may be saying. Who knows, they could have a very good point. If you disagree, say why without attacking the person.

Address the conflict. Even though it may be uncomfortable to do so, the sooner you address the problems in your group, the better. Talk about what you're experiencing. Listen to what others have to say. Are you too critical? Are they truly bothersome? If so, tell them what you need from them in a kind and considerate manner.

Refrain from pairing off with others. Pairing off with other group members might feel good to you but to others it can look like you're trying to gather forces to have your own way within the group. Even though it's probably more difficult, try to engage with the entire group instead of forming alliances with just a few.

Group Roles

Each person who participates in a group functions in a certain role. Some people prefer to take leadership positions while others prefer to follow. They may perform best when given some direction. These roles are an important part of your group's ability to perform its functions. Following are descriptions of the different roles people play in group settings. As you read, think about which role you prefer to take.

Leader. Some people prefer to initiate the action, make decisions, and control how things proceed. They have ideas they want to put into practice. They are comfortable giving direction to people and guiding group outcomes. Leaders often have a big-picture perspective; it allows them to see how all of the different aspects of a group project can come together.

Participant. Some people are happiest when participating in group activities that someone else leads and designs. They don't feel comfortable in a position of control or having the power to set the tone for the group as a whole. They trust others to make those decisions, preferring to help things run smoothly by taking on an assigned role in the project and seeing it through. Participators need to remember that they are "part owners" of the process. Each team member has a responsibility for, and a stake in, the outcome.

Negotiator. Some people sit quietly in the group, listening to the dialogue and observing the group's behaviors, until they know their participation is necessary. Negotiators are good troubleshooters. They can bring clarity to problems and guide the group toward resolutions. These people seem to have an uncanny knack for knowing the right thing to say at just the right moment. They see how things are connected—what people are trying to say or accomplish and how those ideas fit with what others are envisioning.

While each person may have some of the qualities of each of the different categories, more than likely you will have one style that is most developed and comfortable for you. In the following section are tips for each category.

If You Prefer to Lead . . .

Define and limit projects. One of the biggest ways to waste time and energy is to assume that a group will know its purpose and will limit tasks on its own. Help the group decide what needs to be accomplished at a given time.

Map out who will perform which tasks. A group functions best when everyone has a particular function to make. Give people specific responsibilities and trust that they will do their jobs.

Set the agenda. The leader is responsible for establishing and communicating the goal of the project and how it will proceed. Without a plan, it's easy to get off track. Having a written agenda is helpful. A good leader also invites advice from others when determining group direction.

If You Prefer to Participate . . .

Get involved. If a decision you don't like is made by your group and you don't speak up, you are limiting not only yourself but also the group. Your idea may be just what the group needs to hear.

Be organized. When you participate with the group as a whole, stay focused and organized. The more prepared you are, the more likely people will value your contributions and take them into consideration.

Keep your word. Make a difference by doing what you say you are going to do. Your piece of the whole is an important part of your group's success.

Focus on ideas instead of people. One of the easiest ways to engage conflict within a group is to attack a person instead of discussing the ideas with which you disagree. Don't personalize your comments. Instead, stay focused on ideas.

Play fairly. Give everyone a chance to participate. Be respectful of other people's ideas. Don't dominate the discussion or try to control or manipulate others.

If You Prefer to Negotiate . . .

Ask questions. If you see that the participants are stuck, ask leading questions like, "What do you need in order to feel like your ideas have been recognized?" "What does success look like to you?" "If you were required to make this decision for the rest of the group, what would you do?" Get the conversation moving in a new direction—a direction that inspires creative thinking and creative problem solving.

Look for links between participant's ideas. Find the commonality in ideas. If one person is coming at the project from a production schedule perspective while another is discussing costs, point out how the two are interconnected—how length and costs are inextricably intertwined.

Reflect back what you hear being said. Sometimes people don't feel heard in a group setting. If the conversation is moving so fast no one knows whether or not they've been heard, or even what others are saying, slow things down. While people speak, jot down their main points; then, when you can break in to the conversations, share what you hear people saying. Ask for confirmation or feedback to see if you are on target. Doing this allows others to hear the different points more clearly because they are not so busy defending their own point. Help create a listening environment.

The most exciting and rewarding aspect of group work is the moment your team starts performing as a real team. Members are cooperative, creative, and contributing their fair share. When a group is performing well you can expect that the goal is in sight. Enjoy this highly productive, and frequently satisfying, time. Once the project is completed, your group will more than likely disband.

When it's time to disband the group, take some time to celebrate your group's accomplishments. Some groups celebrate by having lunch or dinner together, reminiscing over their process. Others just thank the participants and move on. Still others give small tokens of gratitude. Whatever your style, make sure you acknowledge your team members. You may be working with them again before you know it. The way you say goodbye is a symbol of your ability to be an effective team member.

WHAT ARE LEADERSHIP QUALITIES?

Having and using leadership skills will help propel you into more treasured positions at work and will help you gain more opportunities, in general. You may not want to be a manager, supervisor, or the owner of a business, but developing leadership qualities also will allow you to implement your ideas. If you've never been a leader, think of ways that you can develop leadership skills at work or at play:

- Volunteer to head up a committee at the office or in your community.
- Offer to indoctrinate a new employee.
- Spearhead a new project.
- Start a community block watch program in your neighborhood.
- Offer to coach a young adults sports team.

The ability to influence others in a positive way will earn you respect and keep you in line for promotions. Taking the lead will often command attention from those who are looking for good leaders to move a division or the company as a whole to new levels of achievement. The following sections list qualities that are most often recognized as qualities leaders possess.

Ethics

Most people in leadership positions have proven that they are ethical human beings. They are discreet, value-driven, and respectful of others and the ideals they hold dear.

IN THE REAL WORLD: GUY SHAFER

Howard Erwin Shafer, otherwise known as "Guy," laughs when he describes the best perk of his high-level, executive position with Cudd Pressure Control, a worldwide leader in the oil and gas industry: he gets to have a portable radio in his office!

Raised in a small Texas town, Guy grew up in a community surrounded by ranching. His father, though, had always worked in oil for Exxon Corporation. Ironically, Guy's father discouraged his children from entering into the oil industry, claiming it was too unstable and unpredictable. So Guy went to college at the University of Southwest Louisiana instead. With a football scholarship and somewhat romantic notions of the Navy, Guy thought he had his life all mapped out. But, although he convinced several friends to join the Navy, he himself never enlisted.

> I just didn't know what I wanted to do or be. Still, at fifty-five, I don't know what I want to be. I've always considered myself a little bit of a maverick, but really I just want to enjoy what I'm doing. I would work for free.

After leaving college to get married, Guy went to work for Exxon until he was offered a job with Mobile Oil. In 1963, he explored the supportive network of the oil and gas industry, working in drilling and production. He joined Cudd Pressure Control, based out of Houston, in 1986 as a field representative. He has moved his way up the corporate ladder and was recently promoted to Cudd's executive sales manager, responsible for both international and domestic operations. According to Guy, more good luck comes the harder you work. In his case, it certainly seems to have done just that.

Guy attributes his success to continually learning and increasing his overall knowledge of the oil industry.

> I still learn everyday—I feel like a kid. I have that same excitement I've always had for my job. Sure I could still flip burgers if I had to. I always say I would work for free, and then my wife nudges me and says, "don't forget about the mortgage and food, honey."
>
> I would say attitude is everything in terms of success. I always ask myself, and my employees, "Do you like this job? Do you have fun doing it?" If not, this is America, we are very fortunate here. If you don't like your job, you can switch. If you don't like the industry you work in, you can find a different one. The opportunity is there to do anything you want to do in this country. I've been at the bottom a couple of times, especially in this industry, but I control my own destiny. Sometimes the biggest restrictions we face are the restrictions we put on ourselves.

Commitment

Leaders are committed to success—theirs, as well as the success of those around them. They stay late when they need to, frequently spend personal time learning about the business, and look for ways to increase their effectiveness on the job.

Creativity

Leaders see possibilities, solutions, and the big picture. They rarely get hung up on a minute point. Instead, they inspire others to generate ideas that will move the company or team forward.

Decisiveness

Leaders are able to make decisions when a decision needs to be made. They are not afraid of people's reactions nor a decision that doesn't work out. In both cases, a leader will work with and attempt to resolve any consequences of their actions.

Initiative

Leaders rarely sit back and wait until someone else tells them what to do. Instead, they are self-motivated, excited about accomplishing their goals, and able to motivate others to do the same.

Tenacity

A leader has the ability to step out into uncharted areas. Other people may be afraid to risk looking like a fool or making a mistake; a leader isn't. A leader has courage and persistence when it comes to getting things done.

Without followers, however, a leader isn't a leader. Perhaps the most important aspect of leadership is your ability to get along with others. If your coworkers or employees see you as an inspiration, trust your word, and trust that you want the best for them, they will willingly follow you into uncharted areas. If not, they will resist any attempt on your part to lead them. Be sure that you accept feedback from those you lead. Their comments will let you know if you are on the right track. If you don't ask, you may think that people are in support of you when they're actually not. When you invite feedback, be willing to really hear and respond to what they are saying. Your responsiveness to your followers will establish a trusting relationship—the foundation of a healthy interaction.

Keep in mind that there is a difference between managers and leaders. Managers are people, who by nature of the position they hold, have authority. True leaders do not need to be in any particular position—they influence people because they are trusted.

Marv Freeman considered himself a leader. He was assertive, made decisions easily, and could quickly get people to complete the job at hand. When a management position opened up in his department, he told his boss that he wanted the job. He cited numerous times when he had displayed leadership characteristics—or so he thought. His boss, however, did not agree. Even though Marv felt he exhibited qualities of leadership, his boss said he had failed to gain followership. The people in his office did not respect him, calling him "aggressive and bossy." Remember, leadership requires followership to be effective. In addition, leadership means going the extra mile yourself instead of pushing others to do the work. As you develop your leadership qualities, make sure you are giving yourself valid appraisals.

SUMMARY

Leaders are comfortable taking charge and getting things done even in the face of opposition.

Your abilities to work well with others, contribute your fair share, and lead when necessary are important attributes essential for success in today's business world. In your job, you will be confronted with people from all different backgrounds and lifestyles. Learn to celebrate the differences and the unique perspectives that come from those differences. In addition, develop your group participation skills by volunteering for projects at work. Even though it means you may be putting in more time, the benefit will be a greater proficiency at teamwork and a chance for promotion within your organization.

Each person who participates in a group functions in a certain role. Group roles include leader, participant, and negotiator. Leadership qualities are essential for workplace success today and should be developed. These qualities include ethics, commitment, creativity, decisiveness, initiative, and tenacity. Managers, though given authority through their positions, are not always considered leaders. Likewise, a leader does not necessarily need a position of authority.

Applications & Exercises

8.1 How Do You Participate?

1. What is your learning style profile? _____
2. How does your learning style profile affect your participation in groups?
   _____

3. What can you do to increase your effectiveness in group participation? (listen more, speak up more, etc.)? _____
   _____

4. Think of a time when a group situation was *difficult* for you.
   - What was the situation? _____
     _____

   - Why do you think it was difficult? _____
     _____

   - How did you feel about your participation? _____
     _____

   - Was the group able to accomplish its goals? Why or why not? _____
     _____

   - What would you change if you had the opportunity to do it over?
     _____

5. Think of a time when a group situation was *successful* for you.
   - What was the situation? _____
     _____

   - Why do you think it was easy? _____
     _____

   - How did you feel about your participation? _____
     _____

6. Was the group able to accomplish its goals? Why or why not? _____
   _____

7. What would you change if you had the opportunity to do it over? _____
   _____

8.2 How Do You Deal with Conflict?

1. How does your learning style profile affect your participation in the group when conflict happens? _____
   _____
   _____
   _____

2. What can you do to increase your effectiveness during conflict (speak up about my feelings, ask questions, etc.). _____
   _____
   _____
   _____

3. What behavior from other people causes you the most distress in conflicts? Why? What can you do about it? _____
   _____
   _____
   _____
   _____

8.3 What Role Do You Like to Assume in Group Activities?

1. Are you most often a leader, negotiator, or participant? _____
   _____
   _____

2. What do you like best about your style? Least? Why? _____
   _____
   _____
   _____
   _____

8.4 What Is Your Leadership Style?

The following statements analyze your leadership style. Read each item carefully. Think about how you usually behave when you are the leader and then check the response that most reflects your style. Circle only one choice for each statement. Use the following table for your answers. Total the columns when you are finished.

Once you have totaled each column, you should be able to easily see the areas in which you need to grow in your leadership skills. If you answered *Always* or *Often* most of the time, you are already on the path of good leadership. If not, think of ways you can improve your leadership style.

LEADERSHIP QUESTIONNAIRE

I take time to explain how a job should be carried out.	*Always*	*Often*	*Sometimes*	*Seldom*	*Never*
I explain the part that members are to play on a team.	*Always*	*Often*	*Sometimes*	*Seldom*	*Never*
I make the rules and details clear enough for everyone to follow.	*Always*	*Often*	*Sometimes*	*Seldom*	*Never*
I organize my own work activities.	*Always*	*Often*	*Sometimes*	*Seldom*	*Never*
I let people know how well they are doing.	*Always*	*Often*	*Sometimes*	*Seldom*	*Never*
I let people know what is expected of them.	*Always*	*Often*	*Sometimes*	*Seldom*	*Never*
I make my attitudes clear to others.	*Always*	*Often*	*Sometimes*	*Seldom*	*Never*
I assign others to particular tasks.	*Always*	*Often*	*Sometimes*	*Seldom*	*Never*
I make sure everyone understands their part in the group.	*Always*	*Often*	*Sometimes*	*Seldom*	*Never*
I schedule the work that I want others to do.	*Always*	*Often*	*Sometimes*	*Seldom*	*Never*
I ask that others follow standard rules and regulations.	*Always*	*Often*	*Sometimes*	*Seldom*	*Never*
I make working on the job pleasant.	*Always*	*Often*	*Sometimes*	*Seldom*	*Never*
I go out of my way to be helpful to others.	*Always*	*Often*	*Sometimes*	*Seldom*	*Never*
I respect others' feelings and ideas.	*Always*	*Often*	*Sometimes*	*Seldom*	*Never*
I am thoughtful and considerate.	*Always*	*Often*	*Sometimes*	*Seldom*	*Never*
I maintain a friendly atmosphere on the team.	*Always*	*Often*	*Sometimes*	*Seldom*	*Never*
I do little things to make it more pleasant for others on the team.	*Always*	*Often*	*Sometimes*	*Seldom*	*Never*
I treat others as equals.	*Always*	*Often*	*Sometimes*	*Seldom*	*Never*
I give others advance notice of change and explain the effect on them.	*Always*	*Often*	*Sometimes*	*Seldom*	*Never*
I look out for other people's welfare.	*Always*	*Often*	*Sometimes*	*Seldom*	*Never*
TOTALS	____	____	____	____	____

Reprinted with permission, Chester A. Schriesheim, 1997.

PERSONAL ASSETS

Discovery Through Reflection

On a separate sheet, list as many leadership qualities you can think of within a five-minute timeframe. When you are finished, circle the qualities you possess.

CASE STUDIES

What Would You Do?

One

You have the responsibility of selecting a team leader for the project you created and designed. Because the project is very important to you, you want to make a good choice. The team leader will have the responsibility of managing a team of people ranging in age from 24 to 55 years old. You definitely want someone who can get the project finished in the allotted time and, preferably, under budget. You have three highly qualified employees to choose from and are not quite sure how you are going to decide between them. Look at the three profiles below and then consider the questions at the end of the profiles.

MATT is a 29-year-old electronics expert. He is a "whiz-kid" who shot up the employee ladder with relative ease. Having an easy-going personality, Matt is well-liked by his associates. He regularly goes out for drinks after work or plays ball with them on the weekends. Matt has all the technical skill necessary to accomplish the job. Just like you, he also has many additional creative ideas of his own. He also has a great deal of enthusiasm and tenacity.

KAREN is a 43-year-old woman who has been with the company for just three years. When she was 38, she decided to return to school in order to upgrade her skills. She graduated at the top of her class and has been a dynamic employee since she joined the firm. Karen has many leadership skills. Before she returned to school, she ran her own computer training school, was the president of the PTA for three years, and took conflict resolution classes at her community center. You think Karen would be a good candidate. Even though she's somewhat of a loner and fairly intense, you know she'd have no problem following through on the project.

TONY has the most experience with the company. At fifty years old, he has seen numerous projects come and go. Of the three, he knows the intricacies of the business the best. In fact, he trained both Karen and Matt when they were first hired. Tony has developed many relationships with the different vendors and contractors the company uses. This makes him an invaluable asset to the company. Although Tony is a solid company man, his productivity and enthusiasm for work has waned in the last few years. You wonder if Tony would feel motivated enough to take on a project of this magnitude. But then again, maybe this is just the project he needs to get his motors started once again.

Now answer the following questions.

1. Name the leadership qualities each candidate possesses.

   Matt _____

   Karen _____

   Tony _____

2. Name the main concern you have in hiring each of these candidates.

   Matt _____

   Karen _____

   Tony _____

3. In your interview process, what specific questions would you ask each candidate in order to qualify them for the position?

   Matt _____

   Karen _____

   Tony _____

4. Whom would you choose and why? _____

   _____

Discuss your conclusions with another classmate.

CHAPTER 8   TEAMWORK AND LEADERSHIP   **147**

Two

Your division has been assigned a group project for developing a new product line. You must decide on the product, research whether it is financially feasible, and write a proposal for your superiors to review. Your heart sinks when you realize you are on a team with someone you really don't like. His name is Bob and he has a reputation for being contrary, argumentative, and arrogant. Besides which, he frequently takes off early and arrives late for work. When the group meets for the first time, you realize the entire session was spent listening to Bob's ideas—none of which are interesting to you at all. One of the other members of the group, Sandy, is shy and soft-spoken. You realize she's probably not going to be much help in managing Bob's aggressiveness. Another team member, Chuck, seems annoyed by Bob but has kept quiet so far.

What should you do? Look at the following steps and number them from 1 (most important) to 10 (least important).

GROUP

- B __7__ You find time to have a private conversation with Chuck in order to discuss Bob's behavior.
- G __5__ You speak to your supervisor about your feelings.
- G __2__ You ask each person in the group to bring two ideas for the project to the next meeting so that the entire group can discuss and vote on which product to develop.
- B __9__ You invite Bob out for a cup of coffee so you can get to know him better.
- B __6__ You ask the group to select a project coordinator who can monitor the group's behavior.
- B __10__ You let this session go and hope the next meeting will be better.
- G __3__ You decide that each time Bob dominates the conversation, you will politely interrupt him and invite others to speak.
- B __8__ You decide the best way to deal with Bob is to confront his behavior privately and ask him to cooperate more effectively with the group.
- G __1__ You suggest that at the beginning of the next meeting the group spend time discussing group expectations and procedures.
- G __4__ You call Sandy and Chuck to discuss how you feel and see if they're feeling the same way.

Once you have written in the numbers 1 to 10, form small groups and compare your answers with others. Is there something missing from the list?

Taking Care of Personal Business

Managing Your Health and Your Finances

9

KEY CONCEPTS

- How can you maintain a healthy body?
- How can you nurture a healthy mind?
- How can you wisely manage your money?

Health is not a condition of matter, but of mind.

Mary Baker Eddy

Effectively managing your personal health and finances is important to achieving success on the job. Your body and mind are the tools by which you perform all your tasks. Without healthy physical and mental systems, it will be difficult to meet the demands of any job—let alone a job that pushes those systems to their limits.

This chapter discusses methods for maintaining wellness on and off the job. You will learn how to monitor your health and be able to recognize the warning signs of an overtaxed system. You will learn simple solutions for fueling the body and mind so that you can arrive on the job ready to perform. Finally, you will learn about financial management. Use this chapter as a reminder that your body and mind are the tools that get you where you want to go. If you want to be a success, you'll need to tend to them.

> Last year my father died. Like any person, I grieved for a while. However, I didn't realize how strongly it had affected me. At first, I slept a lot—on weekends, I'd wake up around noon. During the week, I'd be in bed or asleep on the couch by 7:00–7:30 P.M. I'd sleep all the way through to the next morning and still feel tired when I got up at 7:00 A.M. I had always been thin and loved exercise but my exercise soon stopped completely. I started to put on weight and before I knew it, I had put on a whopping forty pounds. . . my performance on the job started to suffer. I just didn't feel motivated or excited about the work anymore. It was a push just to get the basic tasks done. Within a six-month time-frame I had gone from a successful business woman to a person on the edge—I was in real jeopardy of losing my job.
>
> Finally, a friend intervened and advised me to get some help. Thank goodness I listened to his advice. I found a counselor and began to deal with my depression. I climbed out of the pit by learning to talk about my feelings instead of hiding from them by drinking and sleeping. During lunch, I began to walk with another coworker for exercise. My boss noticed a difference and said how relieved she was that I was turning things around. She had been planning on having me take a leave of absence until my health returned. I am so glad I got some help.

Even though this story may seem dramatic, many people struggle to maintain physical and mental health. Every work culture is filled with people who eat poorly, exercise little, overwork, and fail to take care of their emotional feelings. Although companies may promote overwork, the toll it takes will eventually do the company more harm than good. As an effective employee, your job will be to find a proper balance between work and relaxation.

HOW CAN YOU MAINTAIN A HEALTHY BODY?

Most of us already know that eating right, exercising regularly, and getting enough sleep are necessary for good physical health. Even so, many of us have trouble putting these theories into practice. Sometimes, your daily schedule interferes with eating nutritious foods or getting the right amount of exercise. When you've put in a long day at the office and have an event to attend in the evening, you may just want to grab a bite at a fast food chain and eat in the car. Instead of packing a lunch for work, you may have gotten into the habit of eating out. You may be so tired at the end of the day, you just don't have the energy to cook, so you send for a pizza and lay down on the couch to watch television until it arrives. In order to choose health over convenience, though, you have to consciously make health a priority.

Think Health

Catherine Courter, a fitness expert, says: "Before you can make any lasting changes to your lifestyle, you must first establish a mind-set that really believes the change is beneficial. Without engaging your mind, your intention to change will probably be short lived." You can begin by asking yourself if your physical health is more important than the other activities in your life. Is it more important than your job? Is it more important than television? Is convenience more important than health? Of course, your job, the television, and fast food restaurants are not necessarily bad for your health, but, used in excess, they can often hinder healthy habits.

Did you know? The U. S. Department of Agriculture and of Health and Human Services have developed a publication called *Dietary Guidelines for Americans* that lists seven important rules of healthy eating:

- Eat a variety of foods.
- Maintain a healthy weight.
- Choose a diet low in fat and cholesterol.
- Choose a diet with plenty of vegetables, fruit, and grains.
- Use sugars in moderation.
- Use salt and sodium in moderation.
- If you drink alcohol, do so in moderation.

Prioritize

After you have established that health is important to you, you can then decide how to balance your health with the other activities in your day. This can be a very difficult part of maintaining a healthy lifestyle. Pressures and daily demands can interfere or cause you to postpone activities that promote health. Your choice of food can fluctuate depending on your schedule. You may find yourself eating on the run, making do with hotel, airline, and fast foods. You may find yourself entertaining clients over dinner and late night cocktails. Whatever your situation, decide how you are going to incorporate a positive health regime into your daily activities. The following tips come from executives who have learned how to find balance between a busy life and a healthy life:

- **Exercise every morning.** Even though it may be difficult to get up earlier, you'll feel better and have more energy if you exercise.

- **Eat salads or light foods when you're staying in a hotel.** It may be tempting to try new restaurants when you're traveling but you'll be better off if you stick with a simple salad or a light meal.
- **Always travel with exercise clothes.** Be prepared to exercise when you're on the road. Make exercise a habit on the road as well as at home.
- **Use the hotel fitness center or jog around the block.**
- **When entertaining clients, don't drink too much alcohol.** It dulls your senses and creates a poor impression.
- **Bring a lunch to work instead of eating out.** Bring food from home—then you have the assurance that the food that is available is just what you need.
- **Use your lunch time to eat lightly and then take a walk outdoors.** The fresh air can help clear your mind and the exercise will rejuvenate your body.
- **Find a healthy balance between work and rest.** Occasionally, your job will demand that you put in extra hours. When that happens, cut back on your social obligations, not your sleep or your exercise. You're going to need all the energy you have to accomplish your work.
- **Learn to say "no" when it's in your best interest.** If your schedule is becoming too demanding, let go of everything you can and focus on what's most important at the time. In addition, ask for help from others, put off activities that can wait, and focus on the priorities.

Set Reasonable, Manageable Goals

Just as goal setting is an important part of your career, goal setting is equally important in maintaining a healthy lifestyle. If physical health has not been a priority, begin changing your habits one step at a time. Don't jump in so quickly that you burn out within a few short days, or worse yet—cause damage to your body. Instead, approach your new health goals with a plan of action—a plan that works for you. The following tips can be used as guidelines for increasing your physical health:

See a health care specialist. Check with a professional to see if your plan is right for your body. Avoid running to a health food store to buy expensive or unregulated amounts of vitamins or herbs. Instead, visit a naturopath or your family doctor and have them help you establish a plan that is safe and effective.

Make exercise a priority. Instead of driving your car to run errands in your neighborhood, choose to walk. Use the stairs at work instead of the elevator. Work out with a friend and combine your socializing with your exercise. If you have the money, join a health club close to your work or home. Use it regularly.

Get plenty of sleep. Make sure your bed is comfortable and your bedroom is well ventilated. If noise prevents you from falling asleep or wakes you in the night, try using a white-noise machine or ear plugs to block out unwanted sounds.

Watch what you eat. Avoid consuming too much caffeine, sugar, salt, or fats. Instead, give yourself plenty of fruits, vegetables, water, and grains. If you eat meat, choose lean meats and eat them in moderation.

Avoid alcohol, cigarettes, and addictive substances. If you consume alcohol or tobacco, do so with caution and moderation; they are potentially harmful and even small doses can adversely affect your performance.

HOW CAN YOU NURTURE A HEALTHY MIND?

Your success at work depends upon having a healthy mind. Everyday you are asked to think critically about decisions that affect the company as a whole. Without a sharp mind, you will not be able to make as many valuable contributions at work. In addition, the clearer you think, the better you will be able to relate to others. One of the most important skills we can have to help ensure a healthy mind is the ability to manage stress.

Manage Stress

When you hear the word "stress," you may think of tension, hardships, problems, anger, and other negative thoughts and emotions. However, stress can have positive results as well. Stress can be the result of a life change. It comes about due not to the change itself, but to how we react to the change. Victor Frankl, author of *Man's Search for Meaning* and a survivor of Auschwitz concentration camp writes, "Perhaps our last and greatest freedom is our ability to choose how we will respond to any given situation."

When difficulties come our way, we have the ability to respond in different ways. We can let the challenge weigh us down, feeling like we are victims of our circumstances, or we can embrace the challenge as an opportunity to grow. The choice is ours.

Almost any change in life will result in some stress. The Holmes-Rahe Social Readjustment Scale (see the next page), developed by two psychologists. The scale assigns a value to various life changes, which indicates the capability of the particular variables to cause stress (the higher the number, the higher the stress).

Using the scale below, circle the value of all the events that have occurred in your life during the past year. To find your score, sum the values. Scoring over 300 points means that you are at high risk of illness or injury due to stress. If you score 150 to 299, your risk is reduced by 30 percent, and if you score under 150, you have only a very small chance of illness or injury due to stress.

You can activate your sense of control in two ways when you are faced with stressful situations. You may either adjust whatever is causing the stress, or use stress management techniques to adjust the effect that the change has on you.

THE HOLMES–RAHE SCALE TO MEASURE STRESS OF LIFE EVENTS

EVENT	VALUE	EVENT	VALUE
Death of spouse, parent, partner	100	Son or daughter leaving home	29
Divorce	73	Trouble with in-laws	29
Marital separation	65	Outstanding personal achievement	28
Jail term	63	Spouse begins or stops work	26
Personal injury	53	Starting or finishing school	26
Marriage	50	Change in living conditions	25
Fired from work	47	Revision of personal habits	24
Marital reconciliation	45	Trouble with boss	23
Retirement	45	Change in work hours, conditions	20
Change in family's health	44	Change in residence	20
Sex difficulties	40	Change in schools	20
Addition to family	39	Change in recreation habits	19
Business readjustment	39	Change in religious activities	19
Change in financial status	38	Change in social activities	18
Death of a close friend	37	Mortgage or loan under $10,000	17
Change of career	36	Change in sleeping habits	16
Change in marital arguments	35	Change in family gatherings	15
Mortgage or loan over $10,000	31	Change in eating habits	13
Foreclosure	30	Vacation	12
Change in work responsibilities	29	Christmas or holiday season	11

Reprinted from *Journal of Psychosomatic Research*, Vol. 11, No. 2, T.H. Holmes and R.H. Rahe, "The Social Readjustment Scale," 1967, with permission from Elsevier Science.

Keep your promises to yourself and others. Not doing something you promised to do, or not finishing it, can cause internal tension and guilt. Do what you say you will.

Break jobs into smaller pieces. Goals appear more manageable when approached as a series of smaller steps. Perform these small tasks well.

Avoid procrastination. The longer you wait to do something, the more difficult it becomes to do. However distasteful the task may be, getting it done sooner rather than later will alleviate or minimize your stress.

Be thorough. Loose ends can be irritating. Learn to think critically about your work and tie up any minor details before you end the project.

Set boundaries. Learn to say "no" when you have too much on your plate. Speak up for yourself, no one else will.

When the cause of stress lies beyond your control, address its effect on you. For example, if a case of the flu keeps you in bed for a week, call your boss and find out what can be done to keep your workload current. Maybe you can do some work from bed. If not, perhaps another employee can pick up the slack. Manage what you can, and let go of what you can't. Not everything goes right all the time. The world won't end if you miss a deadline. On the other hand, if you avoid dealing with your deadlines in a responsible manner, it will only increase the stress for yourself and those with whom you interact. Be responsible for your life, and it will reduce the amount of stress you feel.

Manage Your Emotions

Your emotional health impacts your effectiveness on the job. Everyone encounters the ups and downs of life. Some people have emotional disorders that interfere with their ability to cope. The following disorders affect people in all walks of life. If you think any of the following pertain to you, seek help and learn to manage your emotions effectively.

Depression. As many as ten percent of Americans will experience a major depression at some point in their lives. A depressive disorder is an illness, not a sign of weakness or a state that can be escaped by just trying to "snap out of it." This illness requires medical evaluation and is treatable.

Post-traumatic stress disorder. Post-traumatic stress disorder (PTSD) may affect people who have gone through traumatic events. While everyone who has gone through a traumatic event does not experience PTSD, many people do. Pay close attention to traumatic events in your life.

Eating disorders. Anorexia nervosa and bulimia are two eating disorders that can have fatal results. Anorexia is the failure to supply the body with nourishment. Bulimia is binging on food followed by purging. Both diseases are very difficult to cure, and professional help is highly urged. In addition, overeating can result in obesity, which is another common eating disorder. If diet and exercise don't help, seek professional help.

Drug and alcohol abuse. Some people can drink in moderation without few if any adverse reactions. Others may become addicted. Pain killers, antidepressants, alcohol, nicotine, amphetamines, and opiates are all potentially addictive substances. Refrain from using them if you can. If not, seek help.

Anger. Anger can be as addictive and as deadly as the substances listed above. If you blow up on a regular basis, can't seem to stop once you've started, and feel better after you've blown, you may have an anger problem. If others tell you that you always seem angry, listen. They're probably right.

IN THE REAL WORLD: PAUL AND TERRY KLAASSEN

"One of our major goals is to break the paradigm that people have about elder care," says Terry Klaassen, executive vice president and secretary of Sunrise Assisted Living. The number of Sunrise Assisted Living facilities has grown to 68 in 13 states since its inception in 1981. Assisted living is a relatively new concept in the United States, and the Klaassens have played a key role in pioneering a new option in elder care.

Unlike the sterile, fluorescent environment in some other elder care facilities, Sunrise offers Victorian-style homes that bespeak luxury and elegance. Sunrise nurtures independence, while trying to protect the dignity and privacy of their residents, and functions as an option for seniors who don't require intense, medical attention.

For the Klaassens, their motivation to develop this type of facility rested in the desire to be of service in their community. This led them to quit their jobs and buy an old house that had once served as a nursing home but was long-since abandoned. They remodeled the home, financing it with the assistance of members of their church congregation and the money they received from the sale of their townhouse. Their goal was to provide an alternative to a nursing home and a more home-style setting for their residents.

Terry first came into contact with the typical institutional look and restrictive feel of a nursing home when, at a young age, she accompanied her father to a local home where her mother was suffering from the final stages of breast cancer. They had no other options for her mother's care at that time.

Paul was amazed that there had been no other options available for Terry's mother. He recalled visiting his grandparents as a child in Holland. They resided in homes similar to those now offered by Sunrise. The elderly are greatly respected in the Netherlands, and rather than shutting them away in the antiseptic environs of nursing homes, they provide those needing minimal living assistance with homes designed more as communities and neighborhoods. The United States had few, if any, facilities that could compare, and the Klaassens made the decision to alter that. "It was a shared vision on both of our parts. There was equal input from both of us, and our strength resided in the fact that we both offered differing perspectives."

When asked about the dynamic necessary to work closely with one's spouse, Terry replies that their ability to work together is grounded in a mutual respect for one another's opinions and feelings and trust in each other's capabilities.

Paul and Terry drew upon their education and personal drive to make their dream a success. Terry recommends that people look closely at their professions. She feels that, in order to be successful, your job should fit your personality. "When you enjoy what you're doing, your motivation is self-perpetuating. Enjoyment of your job is the additional motivator that rises above the monetary reward."

Paul and Terry derive their greatest reward from making a difference in the lives of others. This knowledge provides the foundation that drives the success of Sunrise Assisted Living.

HOW CAN YOU WISELY MANAGE YOUR MONEY?

Many people work very hard to have the money and the material items that make life more comfortable. Popular culture tells us that the more money we spend, the more "toys" we have, the better off we'll be. But is this truly the case? Does money bring happiness, or not?

The first step in managing your financial life wisely is to begin with a philosophy about money. What does it mean to you? If you grew up poor, having money may mean that you have finally arrived at a secure and respected position in life. If you grew up surrounded by wealth, you may view money as a given—something that you will always have. In either case, your ability to think about your financial life will help clarify some of your short- and long-term financial goals. The first step, then, is to think about what money means to you. Ask yourself:

- What kind of income do I need to live the kind of life I imagine for myself? Do I have that income at present? If not, what can I do to accomplish this goal?
- What do I think about credit cards? Are they something that can benefit my life? How? Are there other alternatives I can use instead of credit? What are they?
- What types of savings plans are available? Do I want to invest in my retirement right now or do I want to wait and spend the money on things I need today? Why or why not?
- What is my family's money history? Did we spend easily? Frivolously? Were we miserly? Did we use money as a means to show affection? How has that spending influenced my life today?
- Do I have difficulty asking for a raise? Why? Do I feel I deserve to make good money? Why or why not?
- How do I feel about donating money to worthy causes? Is it easy for me or does it feel like I'm giving and not getting? Do I give to others only when I'm sure there's enough for me?
- What do I spend most of my money on? Entertainment? Basic living expenses? Do I have any money at the end of the month to buy myself nice things? Do I just make ends meet?

One effective way to think about your financial life is to write it down in a journal. If you don't have a journal, take out a few pieces of paper and write out your financial plans and reflections. Use the preceding questions as the basis for your thoughts. When you are finished, share what you learned about yourself with someone else.

Live Beneath Your Means

Spend less than you make. This strategy helps you create savings—it doesn't matter how much or how little you save, as long as you start the saving process. Any amount of savings will give you a buffer zone that can help with emergencies or bigger expenditures. Sometimes the cost of your basic needs will exceed what you make, in which case living beneath your means becomes very difficult, but strive to do this.

Pay Yourself

After you pay your monthly bills, put whatever you can save from your monthly earnings in a savings account. Paying yourself helps you store money in your savings where it can grow. That savings could become security when you grow older, help finance your children's education, help with a financial crisis, or be a down payment on a large purchase. Don't think that the money left over after you pay your bills is automatically available for spending. Make your payment to yourself a high priority. Honor it as you do your other bills.

Plan Ahead

Budget your money with your eyes on the future. Determine how much money you make, how much you spend, what you spend your money on, and whether you need to adjust your spending habits. Think about where you want to be in one year, five years, ten years, and so on. Then adjust your plans accordingly.

SUMMARY

*In order to be successful,
you'll need to treat yourself with respect.*

A person who is able to enjoy life's pleasures and find something positive in its challenges is more likely to have overall success. Treating yourself well, by taking care of your physical and financial well-being, will set you on your way to achieving the success you desire. Managing stress and your emotions will help you nurture your mind and achieve your goals. By living beneath your means, paying yourself and planning ahead, you'll be able to wisely manage your money.

Focus on what is positive and your attitude will affect all other areas of your life. Give yourself the gift of self-respect so that you can nourish your body and mind everyday, in every situation.

CHAPTER 9   TAKING CARE OF PERSONAL BUSINESS   **159**

Applications & Exercises

9.1 Committing to Good Health

Discuss why your health is important, how you would feel if you didn't have your health, and any immediate changes you would like to make. Use this exercise as a chance to reflect on your physical fitness and your personal intention toward your health.

9.2 Managing Your Stress

Review the Holmes–Rahe Scale in the chapter and tally your score. Spend a few moments reflecting on your situation by answering the following questions.

1. What has caused you the greatest stress (according to the chart) in the last year? _____

2. How did you manage this stress (got more rest, saw a counselor, etc.)?

3. When you added up the score, which category were you in (high, medium, low)? _____

4. What can you do to reduce the total amount of stress in your life?

5. What action steps will you take this week to reduce stress? _____

PERSONAL ASSETS

KEEPING TRACK OF YOUR HEALTH

Examine your eating, sleeping, and exercise habits for the following week. In order to get a clear indication of your health habits, try to not change your routines. Instead, go about your activities as usual. Use the three logs to help you keep track. If you need more room, continue on a separate piece of paper.

Food Log

Tally the amounts you eat each day from the different food groups.

	BREADS	DAIRY	MEATS	FRUITS/ VEGGIES	SWEETS	CAFFEINE	HIGH-FAT FOODS	SNACKS
Day 1								
Day 2								
Day 3								
Day 4								
Day 5								
Day 6								
Day 7								

Exercise Log

Write in the types of exercise you engage in for the next week. Be sure and include climbing stairs, housework, yard work, etc.

Day	Types of Exercise	Duration
1		
2		
3		
4		
5		
6		
7		

From a look at the exercise log, evaluate your fitness profile. Are you more or less active than you need to be? Do you need to cross-train? If you could make one change in your physical activity, what would it be?

Sleep Log

For a week, log exactly how many hours you sleep. Indicate when you slept. Include naps and note any waking periods during sleep. Check the appropriate column on days when you felt rested or run-down.

Day	Major Period of Sleep	Waking Periods	Naps	Well Rested?	Run-Down?
1					
2					
3					
4					
5					
6					
7					

- When you felt rested, what effects did your sleeping pattern have on your day? _____

- When you felt run-down, did your different sleeping pattern affect you negatively? _____

- Judging from the information in the table, what seems to be the ideal sleep schedule for you? Describe it here, including number of hours, where you sleep, and when you sleep. _____

Your Food Profile

Look back at the first chart now and see if the food you are eating is affecting your sleep or performance on the job.

- Do you need to increase your activity to compensate for the types of foods you eat? _yes_
- Do you need to cut out coffee in the evening hours because it's keeping you awake? _no_
- Did you overdo your eating anywhere? If so, name the category: _____
- Name one change you would like to make in your food choices. Describe the positive effects you would gain from this change.

CASE STUDIES

What Would You Do?

Candace enjoyed everything about her job except working with her boss. Even though her boss had a solid reputation within the company, he was a workaholic. The demands were almost more than she could bear. While her boss called it the "fast track to success," Candace wasn't sure if the demands were worth the benefits. After weeks of working late and finishing projects at home on the weekend, Candace was at the end of her rope. She just couldn't understand why everything had to be rushed. She believed if her boss actually created a realistic agenda for the staff and herself, people would perform better and probably get the same amount done in the same amount of time—without the headaches. Candace knew she was personally motivated and had high energy. She didn't think she was the problem.

- How can Candace successfully manage this situation?

  Speak with her boss and explain her problem & also let him/her know that too much work slows people down. More stress - poor performance.

- Is the boss being unreasonable?

  Yes.

- Is Candace being unrealistic about today's workplace?

  No

- Discuss this situation with the other members of your class either as a whole or in small groups.

Two

Peter Bradley has been working seventy-hour weeks for the last two months. He knows he is up for a major promotion and wants to demonstrate he deserves it. Peter's wife is upset about the amount of time he is gone from home. Even when he's there, he is so tired he hardly has the energy to talk. Peter's wife also has a demanding career, and she is frustrated at having to carry more than her fair share. When Peter's wife confronts him, he realizes he has been letting her down and agrees to a weekend away at their favorite bed and breakfast. On Friday afternoon, the largest client in Peter's firm calls with an emergency and demands that they meet that evening to resolve the problem. What should he do?

Answer the following questions and then form small groups to brainstorm solutions. When you are finished discussing, share your ideas with the rest of the class.

1. What do you think is the main problem?

2. Do you think his wife should be more patient? Why or why not?

3. Do you think Peter should be putting in 70-hour weeks? Why or why not?

4. Who should come first, Peter, his family, or his job? Explain.

5. How could Peter have avoided a situation like this?

The Road Ahead

Making the Most of Your Career

KEY CONCEPTS

- How do you achieve your lifelong goals?
- How can you advance throughout your career?
- How can you manage failure effectively?

Failure is only the opportunity to begin again more intelligently.

Henry Ford

Why is it that some people can weather great adversity and still find the courage to persevere while others flounder at the slightest challenge? Why are some people successful where others fail? Are the ones who succeed just smarter? Do they have more advantages than others? Think about where you are right now. Just to attend college, let alone finish it, takes something special. The question is whether the attributes of success are unique to just a few, or if we all have what it takes to realize our dreams. The purpose of this chapter is to identify the qualities successful people have so that you can develop and apply them in your own life and career. In addition, the chapter addresses failure. There will be disappointments, of course, but what you do with setbacks will be an important determinant of your success in the long term. Consider Ruth's story:

> Ruth was five years old when she contracted polio. Her doctors told her she would never walk without the aid of a brace on her leg. Instead of accepting the doctor's predictions, Ruth took off her brace in regular intervals and began to practice walking on her own. After months of work, Ruth could walk with a smooth, even stride. She had proven her doctors wrong. But she wasn't finished yet. She decided she wanted to run.
>
> Ruth practiced and practiced until finally she felt ready to enter a race. She came in last. Race after race, year after year, Ruth came in last. Until finally, she wasn't last anymore. She persevered. More time passed, and one day, Ruth won her first race. She kept running races and kept winning, until she finally went on to win four gold medals at the Olympic games.

Think about the dreams you held when you were a child. Did it feel like anything was possible? You may have wanted to be a fireman, a fighter pilot, a ballerina, a mother, president, or have any number of amazing careers. Of course, dreams change and mature just as we do, but we don't have to give up the conviction that we can achieve our goals. We can do almost anything if we dream big and plan for the future. Mary Hammond, vice president of a banking chain, relates:

> I always have had a core belief that I could do anything. I think this has served me very well. It's allowed me to take some steps that to others may have looked like a risk. Instead, I just assumed that I would have what I wanted regardless of when, where, or with whom the opportunity came. I also believed in my work. I love what I do and I think this shows in how I perform. I approach every project with vigor. I don't let challenges get me down. Instead, I look for the solution and the benefits that the challenge offers me. I also produce quality work. I don't accept projects from others that are not up to my standards and I'm equally demanding of myself. I follow the old adage, "if it's worth doing, it's worth doing well."
>
> I can generally see who's going to be a success within my company—they have a certain aura that says, "I can do this and even more." I have a difficult time understanding people who can't seem to get invested in their own success. Maybe they've had too many hardships to overcome, maybe they've never had anyone believe in them so they don't know how to believe in themselves, or maybe success just isn't that impor-

tant—at least how I define success. Whatever the case may be, if people want it enough, I believe it can happen for them if they put their minds and their tenacity to it.

The stories about the achievements of Ruth and Mary are examples of goal attainment. The dreams you hold can be achieved—by doing a little planning, making informed decisions, and having great determination.

HOW DO YOU ACHIEVE YOUR LIFELONG GOALS?

Develop a Positive Mind-Set

Just as children imagine great things for themselves, try to picture yourself accomplishing your goals. Many children have a natural ability to dream big because they have not yet heard anyone tell them that their dreams are impossible. It is after hearing negative messages that we start to lose the ability to dream. Try to get that ability back. Dream big.

Believe in yourself and your capabilities. If imagining success doesn't come easy for you, observe the behavior of people who have achieved success. Observe, and then begin developing some of those characteristics for yourself.

Be willing to work. Hard work can get you where you want to go. If you love what you're doing, the work won't seem tedious. Instead, you'll know your hard work is helping you get to where you want to be. Be willing to put in the extra hours, long weekends, or travel that is required for advancement. Be willing to learn new systems if that's what it takes. Pay your dues and show your employers that you can go the distance.

Learn from your failures and setbacks. Setbacks and challenges are a natural part of the road to success. When your performance appraisal isn't what you want, or your month-end report is returned with editing comments covering the entire page, embrace each challenge as an opportunity to grow and learn instead of viewing it as a defeat. Rewrite the report giving extra attention to the comments. Change the behaviors that got you the poor appraisal. Believe that you can learn from your failures.

Be true to your values. You and your work will be much more respected if you live in accordance with what you believe to be true. If you believe in telling the truth, refrain from telling people what you think they want to hear, but respect their opinions as well. Follow your own values and know that you are right.

Define Success

For some, success is defined as the fulfillment of a particular goal such as becoming a teacher or lawyer, going on a vacation in Europe, or achieving a certain salary. For others, success may be defined as having peace of mind, security, or health and happiness. Your definition of success will be unique to you. How you define success may be completely different than how your family members or friends define it. Define success according to what has value to you—not what others think is important. You're the best judge.

Have a Plan

Although your career plans could change many times throughout the course of your career, having a plan for yourself gives you a framework. Begin by thinking about where you want to see yourself in one year, five years, and ten years. Once you have a general vision of your career life, write it down. The act of seeing it on paper will help you stay focused on your goals.

> "I recommend people review their career goals at least once a year," says career consultant Frederick Short. "I have a personal ritual of reviewing my career and my life in general every year on my birthday. I usually go to a lovely, quiet restaurant, order an appetizer, and discuss the previous year with my wife. I talk about what felt good and what I would have liked to be different. I always take a moment to bask in any special accomplishments I've achieved. I think it's important to celebrate achievements. Then I look ahead at the coming year and set new goals. I've always loved my birthday for this reason. It's like a new year's resolution—the only difference being, I really mean what I'm saying."

Even with a plan, you can fail to accomplish your goals. Make sure that you can assess whether you are meeting your goals along the way. Have measures that let you know whether you are on track such as: "by the age of twenty-five I want to buy a car." When you reach twenty-five check your goal. Were you able to purchase the car or did you need to revise your goal? Why or why not? Were there other commitments that became more important? What were they and why were they more important? Have your values changed as you've matured?

Evaluate your decisions. Before you make decisions on the job, look at how those decisions will impact your career goals. If you decide to go ahead with your vacation plans while your company is in the middle of a major crisis, think about how your absence will affect those with whom you work. Would it be better to postpone your vacation? Think before you act, then, afterwards, assess your actions.

Think Critically

Without engaging your critical thinking skills, you will have a difficult time planning and staying on track. If you don't assess the consequences of your choices beforehand, the end result can be disastrous.

Examine your choices. What are the next steps you should or could take to enhance your career? For instance, if you are deciding whether to accept a position as a regional sales representative, ask yourself if that will take you to your ultimate goal of vice president of sales?

Think about ways to reach your goals. As you go about your work, think about how the things you do are impacting the goals you have set for yourself. Even though you may not want to put in overtime right now, doing so may help you get the promotion you want.

Assess your plans. For instance, if you've decided that your next step should be to apply for the manager position, analyze whether this is the right choice. Take out your last year-end review. Have you made the recommended changes? Do you have the needed skills? If you go for the position, will your supervisor support you? How will the new position impact your personal life? Will you need to work more hours? Travel more? Every change has inherent benefits and challenges. Assess these for each of your goals.

Respect your feelings. Your intuition, or gut feeling, is something you should take seriously. Usually, your instincts are correct and should be heeded. If something feels wrong to you, it may be. One entreprenuer relates:

> When I began at my company, I had the feeling that something wasn't quite right. Call it a hunch or an intuition, I knew that there was something strange going on. But instead of investigating it, I blew it off. There were warning signs all over the place—red flags such as high turnover, whispered conversations in the hallways and cafeteria—but I ignored them. When the company went bankrupt and the owners were indicted for fraud, I wished that I would have listened to the warning bells that were going off in my head. Instead, I had no job and no paycheck to boot. What a disaster.

Generate Support

You will likely need the support of other people in order to achieve your goals. Nurture relationships, network, and get advice as you proceed through your career.

Build relationships. Networking is not about exchanging business cards and expecting favors in return. The act of networking is simply about building relationships with people. Building relationships takes time and effort. By establishing relationships based on trust, commitment, and respect, you make yourself more promotable. Those in management positions will want to know if you can get along well with others. Make yourself "visible" within the company by seeking projects that go beyond the basic job. Make sure, though, that you've done your own work well first.

Network within your field. Learn to keep in touch with others doing the same type of work as yourself. People within the industry can be tremendous resources for advancement. If they have already advanced, they can teach you how to do the same. If they haven't, they can certainly be a support system as you learn to progress. In addition, those within the industry can keep you informed about possible openings in other companies. Stay in touch with those in your field.

Work with a mentor. Although mentoring relationships may take time to develop, they are an important part of your career success. Though your supervisor will act as a mentor as you progress in your job, find another mentor outside of your company or department. Besides giving you moral support, a mentor can connect you with people who can help your career advance, turn you on to trends and innovations in your field, and give you honest advice about your performance. Develop a mentor relationship and rely on it for support.

HOW CAN YOU ADVANCE THROUGHOUT YOUR CAREER?

Determine What Your Employer Wants

If you want to make a career move, begin by looking at the information used in employee evaluations and appraisals. When hired, look at the performance appraisal your company uses. This will likely include

- Your ability to manage objectives (how you handle job tasks, projects, what you've accomplished)
- Your career objectives and the steps you're taking to accomplish them
- The accomplishments of which you are most proud
- Your ability to meet commitments
- Your ability to respond to client's needs
- Your ability to work with others/teamwork
- Your ability to self-manage
- Your ability to handle the technical aspects of the job

One misconception many people have is that the company is always looking out for the employee's best interest. Those who get ahead realize that their success depends on their own actions, and no one but themselves will take the needed steps to put them in a position for advancement.

Chronicle Your Successes in Quantifiable Measures

Note how you have impacted the company in a positive way. Have you brought projects in under budget? Have you developed systems that saved the company time, money, and energy? Have you increased your knowledge by returning to school or receiving special training? Write all of this down and keep the information for your records.

Be Realistic

Occasionally, people think that they are more prepared for advancement than they really are. Do a reality check. How long have you been on the job? If it's just a short while, have you impacted the company in a profound way? Has your work been exemplary? Look to see if others are doing the job as well or even better than you. Have you developed relationships sufficiently to handle the new responsibilities? Will others be able to rely on you with confidence? Be patient and take the time to learn the skills you need.

Develop Your Skills

Continue to increase your marketability. You can do this by volunteering for projects within your department, leading meetings, developing systems that benefit your department and your company as a whole, attending company-sponsored events and training, and working with mentors who can give you realistic appraisals of your skill level.

Ask

When you feel you are ready and have concrete examples to use to defend your position, ask. If you get a negative response, ask for reasons so that you can make the necessary changes and increase your readiness.

HOW CAN YOU MANAGE FAILURE EFFECTIVELY?

Failure and setbacks can be difficult, but they can also provide the impetus needed to make necessary adjustments for your career success. If someone has pointed out a shortcoming of yours or criticized your work, thank them for their honesty and willingness to help you become better. Then change your actions or behavior. If you don't know how to change, ask someone for help. If you don't think you need to change, assess whether the person's comments were warranted. You can do this by weighing the desired outcomes of a project with your performance.

Ask yourself:

- Did I complete the project on time?
- Did I work well with those involved?
- Was the project good quality?
- Did I follow through on the fine details?
- Was I realistic in my assessments of the project (time lines, cost)?
- Were my superiors happy with the end result? Why or why not?

IN THE REAL WORLD: NOEL CUNNINGHAM

Owner of Strings restaurant in Denver, Noel caters to the rich and famous, and to the not-so-rich and famous. An active member of the community, Noel can always be depended on to offer monetary assistance, the use of his restaurant, and simple, old-fashioned energy to those causes near to his heart. Through hosting Mother's Day breakfasts for people in need, sponsoring fund-raisers for the indigent, and donating time and finances to charitable projects, Noel has found a way to make his success work for others.

As a child in Dublin, Noel did not receive a formal education beyond the fifth grade. Instead of going to school, he began an apprenticeship with his uncle, a chef at the Dublin airport. At seventeen, while working in London, Noel decided to pursue education to complement his interests. After completing cooking school, Noel left his ten-year position at the Savoy Hotel to work as assistant chef at London's Berkley Hotel.

When he came to the United States to vacation in California, he liked what he saw and decided to stay. Starting fresh didn't intimidate him at all. It was here that he learned the business fundamentals of operating a restaurant. Working as the chef for a newly opened club, Noel again put his expertise into practice. He spent over five years at The Touch Club, never failing to amaze the owner with his ability to provide customers superior cuisine at reasonable prices, while profiting the restaurant as well.

Noel eventually came to Colorado with the desire to open his own restaurant. Noel learned a dramatic lesson after his partner, who handled all the business and financial aspects of the business, failed to pay the taxes on the restaurant. The IRS came calling, demanding a tremendous sum of money within the space of thirty days. This trying period in his life saw the emergence of Noel's survival skills. He approached banks and suppliers, explained his situation, and asked them to work with him to alleviate the financial strain being put on the restaurant. "I found that the best thing you can do is be straight up with people, and never promise what you can't deliver."

This forthrightness paid off for Noel. Developing his own business strategy through simple trial and error, Noel was eventually able to pay everyone in full. Furthermore, he had gained full ownership of Strings. Noel credits his success to dealing honestly with people, including his staff. "We always listen to everybody. Often, it's the staff's input that makes things happen around here. We are all either equally successful, or equally in trouble."

Noel uses the same philosophy to address other matters in life as well. "My mother created something in all of her children that makes us reach out to those in need. I feel that I am the lucky one, though, as I think that I receive much more than I am able to give. We are only passing through this life. We have to do what we can, and then move on."

Try to keep your spirits elevated even though you may feel embarrassed by your performance or angry at yourself. Everyone makes mistakes. Be gentle with yourself, and learn from your past.

Stay aware that you are a capable, valuable human being. Focus on your previous successes and commit to try harder next time.

Share your thoughts and disappointments with others. Trading stories will help you realize that you are not alone.

Explore why you failed. Although your limitations may have directly or indirectly caused the problem, it could also have nothing to do with you. Whatever the case, analyze why you failed, learn the lesson, and move on.

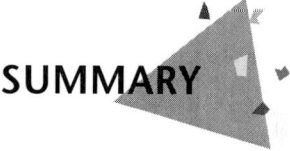

SUMMARY

*Successful people continue learning
and developing marketable skills
throughout their careers.*

Not everyone wants to live life on a fast track to success. We all have different needs and wants. Define success in your own way. To stay current in today's rapidly changing technological world, you will need to anticipate the changes before they occur. Learn about new innovations in the business world. Read trade publications and talk to people who are on the cutting edge of the industry. What trends do they see for the future? Whether or not you want to move up the ranks, continue to grow and learn. Anything is possible!

Applications & Exercises

 How Do You Evaluate Success?

Take a moment to think about your previous year. What did you like about it? What would you change? Give examples of your successes. Were you able to streamline the operation by 30 percent? Did you raise your grade point average from 3.2 to 3.7? Then look ahead to the coming year. What is your vision for yourself? Graduation? A new job? Answer the questions by pairing with another student. Discuss your goals in-depth. When both of you have had a chance to share, write down your goals. As you write, try for career-related answers. If you didn't have a job last year, then use your performance in school or your participation in an organization as an example.

1. Last year, I accomplished . . . _____

2. I felt most proud of . . . _____

3. If I could change anything about last year, I would . . . _____

4. Next year, I want to . . . _____

5. I'll know I was a success by . . . _____

6. In five years, I see myself . . . _____

7. In ten years, I see myself . . . _____

10.2 Self-Evaluation

Think about the last three or four months since you began this course, and then take the following assessment to see how your performance at school has changed since you took the appraisal at the beginning of the course. Have you improved? Stayed the same? Wavered in your progress? Why? When you are finished, revisit your first assessment and then discuss the differences or similarities with another classmate.

1. **Knowledge:** What degree of knowledge have you gained in your different subjects? Would you consider yourself an expert? Do you show interest in learning more?

   Below Average   *Average*   *Above Average*
   1   2   3   4   5   6   7   8   9

2. **Quality of Work:** What attention do you give to your work? Do you check spelling? Have others proofread for you? Turn papers in when they're due? Rework them if they're below par?

   Below Average   *Average*   *Above Average*
   1   2   3   4   5   6   7   8   9

3. **Quantity of Work:** Often gives more than is expected. Is able to help others with their commitments. Helps out in the classroom. Volunteers regularly.

   Below Average   *Average*   *Above Average*
   1   2   3   4   5   6   7   8   9

4. **Attendance and Punctuality:** Arrives on time and is well prepared. If absent, informs those who need to know and asks for help making up the time.

   Below Average   *Average*   *Above Average*
   1   2   3   4   5   6   7   8   9

5. **Flexibility:** Likes working as a member of a team. Finds it easy to change when the situation calls for it. Respects others' opinions. Stands up for own opinion when it matters.

   Below Average   *Average*   *Above Average*
   1   2   3   4   5   6   7   8   9

6. **Initiative:** Has imagination. Not afraid to make decisions. Originates and develops new ideas.

   Below Average   *Average*   *Above Average*
   1   2   3   4   5   6   7   8   9

7. **Planning and Organizing:** Here you show whether you are able to define objectives and set steps to meeting them. How well do you lay out papers? Are you able to stick to your plans? Do you use different resources to accomplish your goals?

   Below Average   *Average*   *Above Average*
   1   2   3   4   5   6   7   8   9

8. **Ethics:** Do you reference other people's work? Do you use your own material? Do you write fresh material or do you draw on papers you've already written? Do you tell the truth about why your paper's late or why you weren't able to finish your part on a group project? How ethical are you?

Below Average				*Average*				*Above Average*
1	2	3	4	5	6	7	8	9

10.3 Looking to the Future

In the following exercise, define what is most important to you by completing the sentences. Imagine yourself in the future, how you want others to perceive you, and what accomplishments you would like to achieve.

1. When people speak about me at my funeral, they will say that I was a person who _____

2. People like me best for my _____

3. Someday, I'll have an award hanging on my wall for _____

4. When the chamber of commerce invites me to be a guest speaker at their yearly banquet, I will speak about the importance of _____

5. Of all the possessions I have, the one I would least want to lose would be _____

6. Every year I donate my money and time to _____

7. I'll know I'm a success on the job when I _____

8. I will have enough money to _____

9. If today were the last day of my life, I would spend it _____

When you have finished, look back over your responses and then answer the following questions.

Are you on the right path to accomplishing your goals? _____

If so, how do you know? _____

What could you do differently, if anything? _____

PERSONAL ASSETS

Mentors

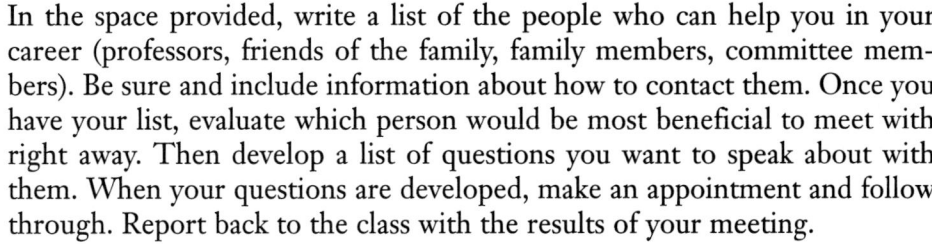

In the space provided, write a list of the people who can help you in your career (professors, friends of the family, family members, committee members). Be sure and include information about how to contact them. Once you have your list, evaluate which person would be most beneficial to meet with right away. Then develop a list of questions you want to speak about with them. When your questions are developed, make an appointment and follow through. Report back to the class with the results of your meeting.

List of Mentors

Name	Contact information (phone, e-mail, address)
_____	_____
_____	_____
_____	_____
_____	_____
_____	_____

List of Questions

1. _____
2. _____
3. _____
4. _____

5. _____
_____

6. _____
_____

WORKING TOGETHER

Tracking Careers

In small groups or pairs, think about the career of someone close to you (parent, friend of the family, older sibling). Discuss the career path they had. Did they get professional training? On the job training? How many times did they change jobs? Did they change careers? What made them successful or unsuccessful in your opinion? How do you think your career path will be the same or different? If you can, discuss the careers of people of different generations (grandparents or children). How do their situations differ from that of your own? Jot down your main discoveries and then share them with the rest of the class.

CASE STUDIES

What Would You Do?

One

You and your team have worked hard for the past four months to complete the development of a new multimedia product. There have been too many late nights and weekends to count. Everyone is exhausted, but you all feel a sense of pride and accomplishment. Several of your team members are experiencing health challenges and another is experiencing family difficulties. Today your boss has asked you to pull your team together for another crash project. The primary product line that produces 65 percent of the company's revenue needs to be upgraded in response to a new competitor's attack.

- What do you do?

- What are the factors that need to be considered?

- Which is more important—your company's success, your team member's well-being, or your need to accomplish your personal goals?

- Is there a way to meet all the agendas?

- If not, what would you do?

Form groups and discuss the issues. When you are finished, using the discussion as a catalyst for your suggestions, write your personal recommendations and discuss these with the larger group.

CLOSING THOUGHTS

Your career journey is an exciting adventure that can be shaped and reshaped again and again. Although you may not feel like the "master of your fate," you have the ability to impact your career by your willingness to grow and change and by the choices you make. Even if your first job is not ideal, use the experience as an opportunity to increase your skills. If you have found the perfect niche, remember to stay current on market trends and develop skill using any new technologies in your field. Finally, continue to use this book as a reference for yourself or as a resource when you are mentoring others.

Remember, more than anything,
your success depends on you!

Index

Accomplishments, 66, 84, 138, 170
Accuracy, 115
Achievement, 8, 11
Action plan, 26
Active listening, 88
Addictive substances, 153
Address, 122
Adult student, 23
Adventurer, 43, 50
Age, 3
Agenda, 137
Alcohol, 153, 155
Alcohol abuse, 155
Ambiguities, 28
Amphetamines, 155
Anecdote, 120
Anger, 155
Antidepressants, 155
Associate's degree, 10
Attendance, 13, 175
Attention deficit disorder, 82
Attitude, 11, 25
Attitude of achievement, 11
Attributes of success, 166
Audience, 118
Awareness, 71

Bachelor's degree, 10, 25
Block watch program, 138
Bodily–kinesthetic intelligence, 44, 49
Body, in writing, 120
Body language, 94–95
Body positioning, 82
Boundaries, 155
Brainstorm, 5, 22, 58–59, 72, 119
Brainstorming, 16, 63–64, 74, 134
Budget, 124, 158
Building relationships, 169
Business documents, 121
Business letters, 122–123

Caffeine, 153
Calendar, 5, 8
Career:
   choice, 51
   goals, 21
   growth, 90

   objectives, 170
   path, 178
   plans, 168
Case studies, 16, 36, 56, 74, 95, 129, 145, 162, 178
Challenges, 167
Change, 2
Choice, 60–62, 69–70, 168
Cigarettes, 153
Cognitive preference, 41
Commitments, 13, 139, 170
Communication, 4, 6, 77–96
   barriers to, 85–86
   basics of effective, 6, 79
   blunders, 116
   breakdown, 80, 88
   challenges, 92
   complex, 78
   conflict resolution, 88
   diverse, 86
   diversity, 85
   effective, 81
   evaluation, 81
   global, 86
   good, 80
   hindering, 79
   in competition, 83
   industry-specific, 78
   interpretation, 81
   listening, 80–81
   managerial, 78
   nonverbal, 78, 82–83, 88, 91, 94
   open, 89
   physical behaviors, 83
   proxemics, 83
   responding, 81
   seating arrangements, 83
   strengths, 92
   style, 10, 92–93
   varied, 78
   verbal, 78
   with respect, 80
Communication skills, 77–96
Community events, 6
Companywide goals, 8
Competence, 69–70
Competition, 40, 125

Computer, 10
Computer technology, 98
Conclusion, in writing, 120
Conflict, 9–10, 88–89, 93, 135, 143
   resolution, 6, 88–89
   style assessment, 93
Constructive criticism, 11, 90
Continued education, 10, 23
Conversation, 83
Cooperative learning, 44
Coordination, 44
Courage to persevere, 166
Coworkers, 64, 85, 140
Creative:
   problem solving, 137
   process, 134
   solutions, 64
   thinking, 57–75, 137
   thinking skills, 6, 41, 66, 134
Creativity, 63–64, 133, 140
   assessment, 65
Credit cards, 157
Critical thinking, 4–5, 41, 57–75, 120
   skills, 135, 168
Criticism, 90
Cultural:
   backgrounds, 79
   issues, 10
Current events, 10
Customs, 10

Daily demands, 151
Daily schedule, 150
Daytimer, 5
Deadlines, 7, 155
Decision making, 59–63, 168
Decision-making process, 62
Decisions, 168
Decisiveness, 140
Department of Natural Resources, 25
Depression, 155
Determination, 167
Dietary Guidelines for Americans, 151
Disappointments, 173
Discrimination, 86–87
Disorders, 155
Distractions, 82
Diverse:
   population, 40
   workplace, 6
Diversity, 3, 6, 40, 85
Documents, 113, 114–130
Drafting, 127
Drug abuse, 155

E-mail, 100, 123–124
Eating disorders, 155
Eating right, 150
Ecosystem, 44
Editing, 121, 127–128
Educational opportunities, 11
Educational software, 74
Effective communication, 10, 77–96
Effective decision making, 59
Emotional:
   disorders, 155
   health, 73, 155
   intelligence, 57–58, 66
   support, 133
Emotions, 155
Employee:
   evaluations, 170
   expectations, 14
Empowerment, 68, 70
   Inventory, 68
Enclosures, 123
Environment, 44
Equal housing opportunities, 87
Ethical:
   development, 4, 7
   dilemmas, 7
Ethics, 14, 138, 176
Exercise, 151–152, 159
Exercise log, 160
Exercising regularly, 150
Expectations, 3–4, 14
Expressing yourself, 77–96
Eye movement, 82

Facial expression, 82
Failure, 166, 171
Fast food, 150–151
Feedback, 90, 138, 140
Field of vision, 83
Figures, 105
Finances, 150, 157–158
Financial:
   goals, 21, 157
   management, 150
   well-being, 158
Fitness center, 152
Fitness profile, 160
Flexibility, 13, 175
Food:
   groups, 159
   log, 159
   profile, 161
Freewriting, 119, 127
Frustration, 135

Gathering information, 66
Gender, 3
Gender-biased, 117
Gestures, 82
Giver, 43, 50
Global:
   communication, 9
   market, 10
Goal, 167
   accomplishing, 23
   clarification, 23
   immediate, 23
   long-term, 23
   setting, 19–38, 152
Goals, 4, 7, 20, 25–26, 28, 51, 152, 154, 165–166, 167, 168–169
   accomplishing, 23, 27, 34
   actions needed, 26
   career, 21, 25
   clarification, 23
   conflicting, 22
   define, 20
   and dreams, 20
   financial, 21, 25
   immediate, 23
   important, 24
   long-term, 20, 23, 25, 34–35
   personal, 20, 25
   reevaluate, 26
   reflect your values, 20
   setting, 19–38, 152
   short-term, 20, 25
   specific, 25
   workplace, 27
   in writing, 25
Grammar, 121, 127
Graphic design, 44
Group, 137
   activities, 135, 143
   conflict, 135
   participation, 142
   process, 133
   roles, 136, 141
   skills, 16
   think, 132, 135
   work, 6, 133, 138
Groups, 7, 83, 132

Habits, 5
Happiness, 168
Hard work, 167
Health, 159
   personal, 149–156
Health care specialist, 152

Healthy:
   body, 149–150
   lifestyle, 151–152
   mind, 149, 153
Hearing loss, 82
Holmes–Rahe Scale, 154, 159

Imagination, 13
In-house training sessions, 10
Income, 10
Independence, 44
Individual objectives, 9
Initiative, 13, 140, 175
Innovations, 133
Instincts, 169
Intelligences, 44
   bodily–kinesthetic, 44, 49
   dominant, 48
   interpersonal, 44
   intrapersonal, 44, 49
   logical–mathematical, 44, 49
   multiple, 44–45, 48, 52, 66
   musical, 44
   naturalistic, 44
   verbal–linguistic, 44, 48
   visual–spatial, 44, 48
Interests, 6
Internet, 10
Internship, 65
Interpersonal:
   relationships, 41, 43
   skills, 10
Intrapersonal intelligence, 44, 49
Introduction, 120
Intuition, 169

Job performance, 16

Knowledge, 13, 175

Leader, 136
Leadership, 131–147
   positions, 138
   qualities, 131–132, 138, 145–146
   questionnaire, 144
   skills, 3, 132, 138
   style, 143
Learning:
   environment, 41
   situations, 55
   style, 39–56, 93, 133, 142
   techniques, 41
Learning styles, 39–56
   active/reflective, 54

assessments, 44
awareness of, 44
bodily–kinesthetic, 45
categorizing, 40
dominant, 40, 46
effective, 40
essential to your working style, 48
factual/theoretical, 54
interpersonal, 45
intrapersonal, 45
inventory, 52
inventory scores, 54
jobs and, 49
knowing, 48
left brain, 41
linear holistic, 54
logical–mathematical, 45
musical, 45
naturalistic, 45
right brain, 41
understanding of, 39, 46, 55
verbal–linguistic, 45–46
visual, 48
visual–spatial, 45
visual/verbal, 54
Learning Styles Inventory, 52, 54
Letter, 120
of acceptance, 127
Letterhead, 122
Life events, 154
Lifelong goals, 167
Lifelong learning, 10
Lifestyle, 21, 86
Listening, 6, 44, 81, 93
challenges, 81
disabilities, 81–82
distractions, 82
effective, 81
environment, 138
responsibility for, 82
skills, 80
stages, 81
Logical reasoning, 44
Logical–mathematical intelligence, 49

Management by objectives, 9
Managerial communications, 78
Managing conflict, 135
Marketability, 171
Material items, 157
Meaningfulness, 69–70
Memo, 100, 123
Memorization, 110
Memory, 105, 107

Memos, 100, 123
Mentoring, 170
Mentors, 171, 177
Minorities, 3
Mission statement, 24, 26, 29, 35
Misspellings, 121
Mnemonic device, 107
Money, 157
Motivation, 10, 44
Multiple intelligences, 44–45, 48, 52, 66

Negotiate, 137
Negotiator, 136
Networking, 169
Nicotine, 155
Nonverbal:
    clues, 84
    communication, 78, 82–83, 88, 91, 94
    skills, 6

Objectives, 8–9, 11, 14, 26–27, 124, 133
On the job training, 178
On-line information, 10
Opiates, 155
Opinions, 135
Opportunities, 25
Organizer, 43, 50
Organizing, 8, 14, 175
Outreach programs, 26

Participant, 136
Pathways to learning, 44–45, 54
Peace of mind, 167
Performance appraisal, 8, 37, 90, 167, 170
Performance review, 37
Personal:
    assets, 35, 52, 73, 110, 128, 145, 159, 177
    growth, 10
    health, 10
    mission, 24
    space, 83
Personality, 41
    spectrum, 41–42, 49, 54
    type, 41, 43
Personnel, 124
Physical:
    behaviors, 83
    fitness, 25
    health, 150, 152

Planning, 14, 175
    process, 24–25
    strategy, 23
Positive:
    attitude, 47
    mind-set, 167
Post-traumatic stress disorder, 155
Prejudice, 86–87
Priorities, 4, 22–23, 33, 35
Prioritize, 151
Problem solving, 44, 66, 72
Procrastination, 29, 33–34, 154
Professional associations, 6
Progress, 69–70
Proxemics, 83
Public speaking, 92
Punctuality, 13, 175

Quality, 115
    of life, 10
    of work, 13, 175
Quantity of work, 13, 175
Question, 103

Read, 104
Reading, 6, 114
    effectiveness, 107
    habits, 110
    retention, 105
    techniques, 108
Reading skills, 97–99, 99–107
    question, 103
    read, 104
    recite, 105
    retention, 105
    review, 105
    scanning, 99–100
    skimming, 99–100
    SQ3R Approach, 102
    survey, 102
Real World, 11, 30, 47, 67, 85, 106, 126, 139, 156, 172
Recite, 105
Relationships, 131–133, 169, 171
Report, 120, 124
Resolving conflicts, 88
Resources, 26
Responsibility, 3, 8
Retention, 105
Retirement, 157
Returning adult student, 23
Review, 105
Revise, 121
Routines, 5

Salary, 10
Salutation, 122
Savings plans, 157
Scanning, 99–100, 102
Schedule, 28
Seating arrangements, 83
Self awareness, 73
Self-confidence, 10
Self-evaluation, 8, 175
Self-mastery, 71
Self-respect, 158
Seminars, 10
Setbacks, 167, 171
Sexist language, 121
Signature, 123
Skill development, 4
Skills, 1–2, 4, 7, 11, 58, 64, 171
    cognitive, 74
    communication, 77–96
    creative thinking, 6, 41, 66, 74, 134
    critical thinking, 135, 168
    emotional, 74
    group, 16
    leadership, 3, 132, 138
    listening, 80
    nonverbal, 6
    other awareness, 73
    reading, 97–107
    self awareness, 73
    speaking, 88
    writing, 119, 128
Skimming, 99–100, 102
Sleep, 152
    log, 161
Small groups, 74
Social obligations, 152
Social Readjustment Scale, 153
Solutions, 9, 59–60, 64
Solving problems, 58, 64
Spatial relationships, 44
Speaking, 44
Speaking skills, 88
Spell checker, 121
SQ3R, 102, 104
Statement of intent, 24
Statistics, 120
Stereotypes, 86
Strategic planning, 4, 23–24, 29
Strengths, 8, 25, 48
Stress, 42, 44, 153–155, 159
    management techniques, 153
Success, 167–168
Suggestions, 134
Summary, 120

Support, 169
   system, 170
Survey, 102

Table of contents, 103
Tables, 105
Team:
   building skills, 3
   leader, 145
   member, 138
   player, 133
   sports, 6
   work, 4, 6, 9, 44, 131–147, 170
Technical skills, 98
Technological innovation, 40
Tenacity, 140
Thinker, 43, 50
Threats, 25
Time management, 4, 19, 28–29, 32
Timelines, 4, 134
To-do list, 8, 28, 33
Touching behavior, 83
Traditional student, 23
Transition from college to the workplace, 1, 7

Understanding others, 77–96

Values, 167–168
Verbal–linguistic intelligence, 46, 48
Vision, 4
Visual learner, 134
Visual–spatial intelligence, 48
Volunteer, 6

Weaknesses, 8, 25, 48
Wellness, 150
Women, 3
Work performance, 41
Workforce, 3
Working full-time, 4
Working together, 16, 35, 55, 74, 94, 110, 128, 178
Working world, 1–3
Workplace:
   objectives, 19, 27
   reading, 97–111
   realities, 1–17
   success, 2, 6
Workshops, 10
Writer's block, 29
Writers'–readers' experiences, 118
Writing, 6, 44, 113–114, 114–130
   accuracy, 115
   analyze your audience, 118
   before you begin, 117
   body, 120
   conclusion, 120
   content, 127
   demands, 125
   drafting, 120, 127
   editing, 121, 127–128
   effective, 115
   elements of, 119
   freewriting, 119, 127
   goals, 118
   grammar, 121, 127
   guidelines, 119
   hook, 120
   to inform, 117
   introduction, 120
   misinterpretation of, 115
   organize the content, 118
   to persuade, 117
   preparation process, 120
   process, 113, 119
   professional, 116
   protocol for, 118
   purpose, 118
   revise, 121
   sexist language, 121
   skills, 119, 128
   spelling, 127
   standards, 125
   state your purpose, 117
   summary, 120
   tone, 115, 127
   transitions, 121
   workline outline, 120

"You" statements, 117